PHILOSOPHY–IN–DRAMA SERIES

VOLUME I

CARTESIAN DREAMS

FORTHCOMING IN THIS SERIES:

PHI-PSI Publishers
Edmonton, Alberta, Canada

P9-EKJ-160

Address all enquiries to: *Permissions*
                                 Phi-Psi Publishers
                                 Box 75198, Ritchie P.O.
                                 Edmonton, Alberta, Canada T6E 6K1.

Canadian Cataloguing in Publication Data
O'Connell, Sean, 1944-
 Cartesian dreams

(Philosophy-in-drama learning series ; v.1)
ISBN 0-9686685-0-X

1. Descartes, René, 1596-1650--Contributions in metaphysics--
Drama. I. Title. II. Series: O'Connell, Sean, 1944 - *Philosophy-in-drama learning series ; v.1.*
PS8579.C66C37 2000   C812'.6   C00-910220-5
PR9199.3.O3175C37 2000

DESIGNER: **SUSAN MUNRO**

COVER ART: **NATALIE NAKONECHNY**

DIRECTOR OF MARKETING & PRODUCTION: **PAM EYRE**

PRINTING AND BINDING: **SWARM ENTERPRISES**

Front cover painting: Pretty Septic. Natalie Nakonechny. 30"x36" (Acrylic)

Φ–Ψ

PHI-PSI Publishers
Box 75198 Ritchie P.O.
Edmonton, Alberta, Canada
T6E 6K1

CARTESIAN DREAMS

A PLAY IN TWO ACTS

BY

SEAN O'CONNELL

$$\Phi-\Psi$$

CONTENTS

PHILOSOPHY–IN–DRAMA SERIES

VOLUME I

PREFACE TO THE SERIES

The first great Western Philosopher and one to whom all others bow – if not in agreement then at least with reverence – wrote nearly all his works in quasi-dramatic form. Plato's dialogues are theatricised conversations between his teacher Socrates and a host of adversaries, auditors, and associates. Although they were never intended to be pure dramas like those of Euripides or Aeschylus they do manifest a few dramatic elements of setting, plot, and character. While Plato's purpose was never to representatively portray human action or motivation, he certainly believed that dialectical exchange was not only the highest level of philosophical activity and the best philosophical method but quite evidently the best medium of exhibiting and explaining abstract philosophical concepts, theories, and arguments. Other stellar philosophers, most notably David Hume and George Berkeley, seem to have agreed with Plato on this point.

On the other hand great playwrights appear to be exploring perennial philosophical concerns in a purely theatrical medium and in a non-didactic way. Plato, Hume, and Berkeley want to edify and persuade with discursive reasoning while dramatists want to express and explore with theatrical devices. But what the dramatists express and explore, mainly, are traditional problems in philosophy: moral, political, and metaphysical problems experienced in existentially specific plots and characters.

In my brief and undistinguished career as an actor I did roles in Shakespeare, Ibsen, and Miller. I noticed that although these and other authors were not "doing" philosophy they were undeniably preoccupied with philosophical dilemmas and issues. Questions about personal identity, ethics, rationality, religious faith, political authority, gender politics, and epistemology are raised and dramatically investigated in these three writers and countless others who write in the same genre.

The five plays in this series represent my attempt to synthesize the aspirations of pure philosophy and the aspirations of pure drama at some level that transcends and incorporates each of them. What first moved me to make this attempt was a remark by the German Romantic philosopher Schelling that "Art is the organ of Philosophy". Nietzsche augmented Schelling's insight when he said "The more abstract the truth that you would teach the more you have to seduce the senses to it". These remarks gave me two related reasons for combining philosophy and drama.

What did Schelling mean when he said that art is the organ of philosophy? He probably meant that art is the best medium or tool available to philosophy for asking and answering its questions. If this is what he meant then most philosophers would find the remark either scandalous or naïve. The instrument or medium is of course reason and conceptual analysis, not imagination and aesthetic expression. That is why Aristotle's magnificent system of logic is titled *The Organon. The Organon* describes the methodological *tool* with which philosophers must carry out their operations of constructive and destructive argumentation. The *organon* (instrument) is logic, and logic is a formal system of precisely defined rules for valid and cogent reasoning. How, then, can art be the organ of philosophy? If Schelling is right then most philosophers must be wrong when they describe what they think they are supposed to be doing when they are doing philosophy.

In one way or another the five plays in this series end up on Schelling's side.

Each play somehow agrees that philosophy's traditional canons of logic have been and *ought* to have been displaced by some other canon (probably though not necessarily an aesthetic one). Schelling's view has attracted some impressive company. Logical Positivists and their contemporary descendants, existentialists, and pragmatists agree at least that classical philosophy made promises it did not and *could* not keep. And scores of loosely called post-philosophical, post-modern thinkers believe what poets, playwrights, novelists, painters, composers, and so on, have assumed all along: The deep puzzles and mysteries traditionally confronted by philosophy simply do not yield to deductive reason. Perhaps they do not yield to anything. Perhaps they can only be expressed and explored aesthetically. Their agonies can be transmitted – imaginatively, emotionally – in formalist or representational ways without ever being resolved.

What did Nietzsche mean? He undoubtedly would have agreed with the spirit of Schelling's proposal but his claim goes beyond Schelling's. Nietzsche agrees that philosophy must find a new form of expression and a new medium of investigation but he extends his claim to *teaching*. The more abstract the truth that *you* would *teach*, he says, the more you have to seduce the senses to it. The senses can be seduced in many ways but paramount of all these ways for Nietzsche is ART. And art, says Picasso, is the lie that helps us recognize the truth. To appease Nietzsche, Picasso should not have said *the* truth but *your* truth. Still, the main consideration is pedagogical. Art is our most powerful teacher – something Plato recognized long ago.

Prompted by Schelling and Nietzsche, I have tried to simultaneously accomplish two things in these five plays. I have sought to produce dramatic philosophy and philosophical drama. I mean, I hope to have produced in all five plays something which will stand on its own aesthetically, independent of its pedagogical value, *and* on the other hand I hope that each play will reflect

Plato's desire to reproduce the dry processes and results of philosophical preoccupations in a lively, entertaining medium. Hence if the plays succeed they will be decent art containing philosophy and they will be decent instruction in philosophy presented artistically.

Cartesian Dreams was my first attempt at playwriting. This was followed by *Lives and Evils,* then by *Neecheemoos and Inuspi* and then by *Winter at Delphi. Plato's Retreat* was written last in the series. After completing *Lives and Evils* I detected an increasing didacticism in that play compared to *Cartesian Dreams. Neecheemoos and Inuspi* represents a conscious reversal back to the pronounced aestheticism of the first play. This attempt to balance pedagogical and aesthetic interests has brought to light what is now for me the greatest challenge in writing, namely, to heartily endorse Schelling's dictum and Nietzsche's mortifying demand. If it is true that the more abstract the idea the more sensuous must be its representation then the task of representing the most abstract ideas must be an impossible one. Abstraction and aesthetic sensuality seem to be antipodes: like a negative correlation each factor seems to recede as the other increases. Finding a synthesis of abstraction and sensuality, of didacticism and aestheticism, has been the source of my greatest despair and my greatest delight. I have published some pure philosophy and some pure poetry. Each of course has its own peculiar demands and difficulties. Neither, however, presents the challenge of poeticized philosophy. I trust I have overcome these challenges to some degree, at least to the extent that the abstract and the didactic do not lose their conceptual sharpness and logical rigor when they are transduced into poetry and that the sensual and poetic do not lose their aesthetic charm and artistic expressiveness when they are laced with logic.

Indeed, I still do not know if *Cartesian Dreams* floated into my awareness as philosophy theatricised or as theatre with philosophical content. Descartes, struggling with his doubts about whether or not his senses might be deceiving him, suddenly presented himself as a perfect character for drama. I knew that he belonged in theatre (perhaps vaudeville), as did the quirky Queen Christina of Sweden. How could a writer not put these two absurd, comedic, and tragic characters on stage together? So I did and most of my students loved it. I was hoping they would read *Cartesian Dreams* in order to better understand Descartes' *Meditations on First Philosophy* but to my surprise many of them read Descartes in order to better understand my play. At that point my project was born.

Truthfully, I thought I was just appropriating two brilliant and fascinating historical characters from the world of letters for the purposes of art. As the play slid off the tip of my pencil, however, I realized that its two lead protagonists were locked as much in philosophical labor as they were in love's toil and turmoil. Art and philosophy were inseparable from the outset.

Lives and Evils is much less theatrical than *Cartesian Dreams*. It was consciously written for teaching purposes, inadvertently sacrificing aesthetic intensity to pedagogical practicality. It was in writing this second play that I became fully conscious of the tension between didacticism and aestheticism: the excluded middle of either/or became a tantalizing temptation (since neither/nor is not in my vocabulary). The project was almost abandoned: either art or philosophy but not both. But Nietzsche, whom I damn and praise in his incendiary brilliance and prodigious febrile talent, kept taunting me. The result was *Neecheemoos and Inuspi*. I set out to write this play with the extreme aestheticism of *Cartesian Dreams* in mind and the reactionary didacticism of *Lives and Evils* in mind. I had hoped to write a play which in being read or viewed would leave pedagogy and art indistinguishable. I thought I had fusion. But readers of *Neecheemoos and Inuspi* (which, I add, is my favorite play of the five) frequently said they did not know what the play was "about". Evidently I did not have the synthesis I thought I had. Consequently, of the two plays before it and the two after it *Neecheemoos and Inuspi* was the only play to have been thoroughly rewritten so it would be more "about" something studied in philosophy courses. *Plato's Retreat* was gutted and rewritten so it would be *less* "about" something. All in all I believe that in each play the no-man's land on the terrain of excluded middle between 'either' and 'or' was stormed and bridged from opposite directions. After *Neecheemoos and Inuspi* came *Winter at Delphi*, a strange mix of classical mythology, grand opera, burlesque, and the foundations of philosophy – not to mention philosophy's justification. Philosophy is actually put on trial in Athens. *Winter at Delphi* and the re-write of *Plato's Retreat* were both (I trust) written while I was camped on the Lawn of Included Middle – something demanded by Art but prohibited by Logic.

Two features strike me as I review the evolution and content of these plays.

First, I make few philosophical assertions of my own in the first two plays but more through the last three. *Cartesian Dreams* and *Lives and Evils* are philosophically inconclusive. They chart philosophical territory but no claim is staked. By the end of *Winter at Delphi* and even more clearly by the end of *Plato's Retreat* I give the philosophical content of the play an authorial stamp of approval or rejection. I make no apologies for that. It means only that whether or not my conclusions in philosophy are interesting I am increasingly using art as a medium for constructing my own philosophical judgements.

Second, and far more interesting, is the fact that all these plays are at bottom about love. If there were one thread to make a quilt of these plays it would be love. If find it astonishing and you will find it unbelievable that it was never my intention in *any* of these plays to write a love story. They just fell into place that way. Descartes and Christina are mystified by love as they discuss metaphysics; Plato and Erothymia are consumed by love while working out a theory of justice; Neecheemoos sips nightly love potions with the man she loves while raising questions about the epistemological foundations of the European civilization that displaced her own; a fallen gay priest ponders the mysteries of love and lust while teaching theodicies, and so on. This thematic continuity, though, is not as interesting or significant as the then-unconscious thoughts which caused it. Certainly the plays can be read at one level as love stories and nothing more. I have to ask myself, however, why these different plays on such diverse topics as the mind-body problem and the problem of evil should all have been plotted around love. The answer is found in the leading female character in each play.

Over its two-and-a-half-thousand year history philosophy has been a labor of reason. Systematic logical and conceptual methods have been deployed by philosophy in its assault on mystery. Arbitrarily, the official beginning of philosophy has been set around 585 BCE, when the polymath genius Thales asked questions about the first principle of the universe. He asked a stunningly original question in what we now call metaphysics. Equally stunning, though, was the way he answered it. He asked "What is the *arche*?". What is the basic stuff, or cosmic substance, underlying and supporting the multifarious, changing things we witness with our senses? What is the unchanging *reality* out of which the world was made that supports the *appearances* it generates? Thales is identified as the first philosopher because he tried to answer his question not by going to oracles, not by repeating Greek myths or traditions, not by consulting poets, but by constructing logical arguments based on public evidence. He used *objective* evidence available to everyone to form a conclusion testable by anyone according to rational criteria. Mainstream philosophy since then has furthered Thales' ambitions by using impartial, objective, rational methods to answer the most basic questions about the universe and the place of humans in it. Was the universe created? If so what was the agent of creation? Do humans possess a non-physical aspect which can survive bodily death in a disembodied state? If so, how is that aspect connected to our bodily aspect and what happens to it after it is disconnected? If not, what is a mind and a person? What are the limits of what we can know? What is the best possible life? What are the best rules to abide by collectively to maximize goodness in our lives? Who should make and enforce these rules?

A most startling fact about the labor of reason is that until very recently it has been carried out almost entirely by men. Even skeptical critiques of reason (themselves eminently reasonable) have come almost exclusively from men. Explaining why this is so requires deep and careful thinking that goes far beyond jejune feminist notions of 'oppression' and so on. I shall not pursue any explanation here. I only wish to notice that the history of philosophy has been the history of reason at work on puzzles, questions, and mysteries beyond the scope of natural or social science and the most enduring and important work in this area has until recently been done by men.

The fact is that male philosophers, great and not-so-great, have largely neither understood women nor have they enthusiastically courted their advice in metaphysics and epistemology. Even Plato in his qualified argument for gender equality thought of capable women as diminutive men. Aristotle thought of them as rationally defective. Greek culture, however, wisely made a female Goddess the patron of Wisdom. And philosophy is the love of *that*.

I ended up with love stories in all five plays and I note with surprise that each plot pivots around a strong female character who while not perfect has something more to teach the male character than he has to teach her. Usually she has to teach him that rationality has its limits. Christina, Sophie,

Neecheemoos, Erothymia, and Athena all share a deep respect for the potent instrumental efficacy of logic and science. Not one of them is foolish enough to deny objective reason its rightful and demonstrated value as a distinctly human capacity. But each assigns reason to a subordinate or at least cooperative role in relation to the other distinctly human powers that each of us must bring to bear on the issues and questions pressing upon our human subjectivity.

I could speculate on why this insistence on limiting rationality comes consistently from women but I would prefer to let the female characters speak for themselves. I would note only that these anti-Platonic and anti-Cartesian women speak their minds to Plato, Descartes, and others from an eventual position of clarity and strength. Moreover they speak from *love* to men they regard as rare heroic geniuses. Misguided geniuses, perhaps, with their devotion to logic in metaphysics, but rare and heroic nonetheless. There is no doubt that all these women love intensely and that by each play's conclusion they are powerful, centered, competent women. There is equally no doubt that their clear and solid love is what eventually leads their philosophically overweighted men to stances which reason could not provide them. In some cases the female characters must first discover or possibly recover their wholeness as *women* before they can guide their intellectual titans. Christina and Erothymia must first demonstrate their intellectual superiority – after all they are squaring off with Plato and Descartes. Having planted their feet solidly on *terra firma feminae* Erothymia and Christina then fertilize but sharply delineate their love's logic, supplementing but not displacing reason with powers and capacities formerly feared and misunderstood by both Plato and Descartes.

I believe that their fear and misunderstanding of lust, love, and passion led Plato and Descartes to unintentionally write some of the most comical material in the history of western Philosophy on those subjects. Descartes on the passions is hilarious. That is because while he probably loved a few women and respected most others he never understood them and so never learned a thing from them. Why is it that for Descartes the mind-body problem is metaphysical while for Christina it devolves around what to wear: a bikini or a suit of armor? And why is it, in *Lives and Evils,* that Sophie is more concerned to hold the philosopher's hand while he dies of AIDS than to solve the theoretical problem of evil and suffering?

Whatever the answer, the central female characters in these plays do not want to become imitative duplicates of the men they love nor *would* they even if they wanted to. They *add* something distinctive to masculine philosophy. They do not usurp or belittle it nor do they capitulate to it. They supplement it and in so doing modify it. With this aspect of my plays I am extremely happy. To ignore women like Christina, Sophie, Neecheemoos, Athena, and Erothymia will leave philosophy arrested and deformed. I love each of these intriguing women – they have in common some superlative qualities for which I have nothing but reverence. I would happily be led and loved by any one of them, although to me the most fascinating of the five is Neecheemoos.

Neecheemoos, which means 'dear one' or 'sweetheart' in Cree, incarnates thousands of years of windswept wisdom in her aboriginal hair and blood. She is illiterate but glowingly intelligent and intuitively profound. She knows nothing about science, logic, economics, or arts and letters. Moreover she doesn't need or want to. She just loves Inuspi and his strange European ways. She knows that Inuspi (the Cree name for her Irish husband) is ill and that his sickness is nothing less than western civilization itself – the very sickness which eventually killed her. She possessed, in Inuspi's words, "the most beautiful heart that was ever broken". She represents the aboriginal spirit and culture that was violently uprooted and displaced by European colonialism and its attendant evils of greed, cultural imperialism, environmental degradation, technical domination, and spiritual scholasticism. Her remarkable femininity, unadorned by rhetoric and academic pettifoggery, is an unwavering indictment of western epistemology, metaphysics, ethics, and politics. Inuspi, as well-intentioned and as far ahead of his time as he was, realizes too late that everything he needs to cure himself of his pathology went with Neecheemoos to her grave. If western philosophy had only one of the five female characters to listen to I think it should be Neecheemoos. She could barely speak English, and Inuspi spoke in halting Cree, so together they invented a new language (and with it a new state of mind), the language of the love-land Keyamawisiwin, in which the western categories of capitalistic acquisition, sin, egotism, institutionalization (of law, medicine, education, and religion), and repression dissolve into the informal tribalistic laws of happiness engendered from the earth, the heart, the genitals, and when it is appropriate the head. Male philosophers and those female philosophers who are trying to become what male philosophers should no longer be ought to take a deep draught of Neecheemoos's potion Okimawask: that-by-means-of-which-we-love-each-other. The ingredients of Okimawask are a secret, known only by women.

CARTESIAN DREAMS: INTRODUCTION

Cartesian dreams are the sort of dreams one would expect a Cartesian to have. *Cartesian* means anything associated with or derived from the thinker Des*cartes*, for example the Cartesian coordinates of analytical geometry, of which Descartes was the founder.

Rene Descartes ushered in the modern age of Philosophy at about the midpoint of the seventeenth century. His influence was enormous in many fields but his philosophical influence was mainly in metaphysics and epistemology. He defined the questions in these two areas that preoccupied philosophy for the next three hundred and fifty years. What can be known with certainty and how is it known (epistemology)? What are the elementary substances out of which all reality is constituted (thought by Descartes to be mind and matter) and how do these two basic kinds of being relate to each other (metaphysics)?

Descartes was obsessed with discovering foundational certitudes upon which he could construct a system of indubitable beliefs. The foundational certitudes had to be incorrigible, that is, resistant to all conceivable doubt. He wanted his most fundamental beliefs to resist not only all *reasonable* doubt but all *possible* doubt as well, meaning that they could not even *in principle* be false. This kind of certainty could be called 'philosophical' certainty. Upon analysis it will turn out that very few, if any, of our beliefs are philosophically certain.

Psychological or subjective certainty is not philosophical certainty. Subjective certainty is a more or less intense feeling or inner conviction that one's belief is correct. I may have an obstinate subjective devotion to the belief that last night God spoke to me. It is obvious that I cannot be philosophically certain that God spoke to me, however. The content of the claim about which I am subjectively certain *could* be false, and the faintest possibility that it *could* be false is sufficient to make it less than philosophically certain. As long as I can adduce even *one* consideration which makes it theoretically possible or conceivable without logical contradiction that the belief *might* be false then I must admit that it is not philosophically certain. Coming up with such a consideration is not hard to do. It is possible for example that my flu-induced fever caused me to hallucinate a voice I mistakenly believed was God's. Or I might have been dreaming the voice. I do not need to know that is was true that I was hallucinating or dreaming, I need only to entertain one or both of those possibilities to make the belief less than philosophically certain. Whether the probability is very high or very low that I was only dreaming the voice does not matter. As long as it is logically possible that I was dreaming – at whatever level of probability – then I cannot be philosophically certain that God spoke to me.

It is important to notice that I may be very sincere in my belief that God spoke to me. I may even be willing to suffer ridicule, indignity, or persecution for persisting in my belief. But that does not affect its philosophical status: it is still theoretically uncertain. Hence I can have a high degree of subjective certainty about something to which I can attach no philosophical certainty whatsoever. Indeed, a high degree of subjective certainty about something that bears no philosophical certainty is sometimes a sign that a belief is being held for emotional or psychological reasons that the believer is afraid to investigate. Lovers and gamblers are often prone to this kind of stubborn subjective certainty. Philosophy has no interest in it.

It is also important to notice that the considerations which render a belief less than philosophically certain may be trivial and outlandish. Anything, no matter how wild and improbable, that can make a belief philosophically uncertain will do. For example, nobody seriously believes that the universe came into existence only eight minutes ago. But can we be philosophically certain that it didn't? No we can't. It is very unlikely, but there is an infinitesmally small possibility that everything instantly came into existence only eight minutes ago, including fossils, ancient manuscripts with thousand year-old dates on them, buildings in a state of decay, and humans at various stages of development. And of course our *memories* might have been created only eight minutes ago. Until that possibility is proven false, we would have to remain philosophically uncertain about the age of the universe. Curiously enough it cannot be done. We can refer to nothing in the universe to disprove the possibility that it is more than eight minutes old, since whatever we refer to will be part of the universe and consequently it too is subject to the doubt that it is no more than eight minutes old.

There is another kind of certainty we all share and which none of us could do without, but it is still not the kind of philosophical certainty Descartes seeks. A good name for it would be practical certainty (from the Greek *praktikos*, concerned with action). It is the species of certainty on which we act without theoretical reflection or awareness. I have, for instance, a practical certainty that the pill I take from a bottle has the same ingredients in it the label says it has – even though I could be wrong. Practical certainties are just cognitive habits. We do not bother to prove them because we don't feel the need to. It is a practical certainty, for example, that every event has a cause. Nobody has much emotional attachment to this belief and nobody questions it at a practical level. We unquestioningly assume it for the purposes of doing and acting. When we want to get a stalled car running or when we want to change someone's behavior we think without hesitation that the car's stalling or the person's behavior has a specific cause. We are *subjectively* and *practically* certain that every event has a cause even though we may be able to think of reasons for not being *philosophically* certain of it.

Two practical certainties have been of great interest to philosophers. One of them is that the future will continue to resemble the past in all important respects. We are practically and subjectively certain, in everyday life and in science, that all the past laws of gravity, thermodynamics, genetics, biochemistry, behavior, and so forth, will still be in place tomorrow. David Hume has shown, however, that we cannot be philosophically certain that tomorrow's laws will be the same as today's. The sun may have risen in the east every day in the past but that is no guarantee that it will do so tomorrow. We will be practically certain of it though and pull the shades on the east-facing windows at night.

Another practical certainty (to which we attach a high amount of subjective certainty as well) is of greater interest to Descartes. It has been described by one writer (Feldman, 1986) as Locke's Hypothesis, named for the father of British Empiricist Philosophy, John Locke.

> *Locke's Hypothesis: In standard cases of perception, sensations*
> *are caused by objects outside the mind that generally resemble*
> *the ideas of those objects.*

It is an everyday, commonsensical, unquestioned practical certainty that what we think we normally see, feel, hear, taste, and smell is caused by stimuli external to the mind which are really the way they seem to us to be. That is, in "standard cases". I may be dreaming that I am looking at a cloud, or I may have a drug-induced hallucination of a cloud, or I may have been unwittingly wired up with electrodes to think I am experiencing a cloud, but in each of these cases nobody would say that I am actually seeing a real cloud. These are not "standard cases". In a normal situation, though, when I look up and have an experience of white billowy things against a blue background I am practically certain that what I am consciously aware of in my mind accurately portrays or corresponds to or represents something external to my mind, and that what is external to my mind is really the way it appears to me to be when I am experiencing it. I am also practically certain that the cloud I perceive would exist even if I were not experiencing it or even if no one were experiencing it. Nobody doubts this at a practical or subjective level. We all assume there is a world out there independent of our minds and we assume it is roughly the way it seems to be when we sense it under normal conditions.

These two practical certainties, that the future will resemble the past and that there is a world external to our minds which causes and resembles our private experiences, are not philosophically certain. It is *possible* (conceivable without logical contradiction) that gravity will stop operating tomorrow. It is possible that the cloud I think I see is either not there at all or not there in the way I think it is. However improbable these possibilities are does not matter. So long as I can conceive the possibility that gravity will cease operating or that the cloud is not there, I cannot be philosophically certain about either of these things.

Descartes was interested only in philosophical certainty. He wanted to be philosophically certain beyond all conceivable and possible doubt that his elementary and foundational beliefs were true, such that any beliefs derived from those basic beliefs would be anchored in a secure and philosophically unshakeable footing. He wanted his foundational beliefs to be indubitable – not beyond subjective doubt, not beyond practical doubt, but beyond speculative, theoretical, philosophical doubt. He wanted to be infallibly sure that it was *impossible* for his foundational beliefs to be *false*.

What better way to achieve this than to doubt everything until you find something immune to all theoretical doubt? Something that, no matter how hard you try to think of reasons for it to be philosophically uncertain, resists every attempt? Or even more strongly, something that verifies itself in every attempt to doubt it? This is what Descartes does in the opening section of his famous *Meditations on First Philosophy*. He decides to subject all his foundational beliefs to theoretical doubt. He does not ask if he feels uncertain or psychologically uneasy about them. Nor does he ask if he should suspend his practical allegiance to them. He asks if there is any conceivable reason to think that they could be false. Whatever is conceptually doubtful he will not believe. He will try to out-doubt the most radical skeptic using the most extravagant thought experiments, so that whatever survives what he calls his "hypothetical" doubts will be philosophically certain even to the skeptic. His hope is that he can turn the skeptic's tool of doubt against skepticism itself and defeat skepticism with skepticism. I get an image here of Descartes in an epistemological demolition derby: He will attempt to annihilate everything in sight until either everything is in ruins or something is left standing which resists every attempt to pulverize it.

Descartes wastes no time in getting down to philosophical business. He goes right for Locke's Hypothesis, finding that it is not philosophically certain. Can Locke's Hypothesis be doubted? Let's see. Recall that this is a hypothesis, hence it *alleges* that we have a certain kind of mental event called a perception. A perception is commonly thought to be a direct apprehension of extra-mental and mind-independent reality. It is usually supposed that the world is perceived through the channels of sense experience in which sensations of such things as redness, acidity, shrillness, hardness, putrescence, and so on, are bundled together into a perception. And it is thought that when our perceptions are not distorted by fatigue, chemicals, desire, fear, hypnosis, mental illness, and so on (which is to say in "standard cases of perception") the sensations we have of redness or sweetness or whatever are caused by objects outside the mind. By 'outside the mind' Locke means that these objects exist in their own right and are in no way dependent on being perceived by minds for their existence. The hypothesis further *alleges* that the sensations we have are duplicates or mental xeroxes of properties inherent in the objects themselves. Descartes wants to know if he can be philosophically certain about the two central claims in Locke's Hypothesis. He want to know if he can he be sure, first, that our sensations are caused by extra-mental objects and he want to be sure, second, that (if our sensations are caused by extra-mental objects) the sensations we have of them are accurate depictions of the objects themselves. In the preliminary stages of the *Meditations*, Descartes simultaneously takes on both aspects of the hypothesis.

Can we be philosophically certain that our sensations are *always* faithful portrayals of external objects? Of course not. Our senses often deceive us. Imagine driving down a highway on a hot day. About a mile ahead there appears to be a pool of water on the highway. But on reaching that spot the road appears to be perfectly dry. The same spot could not be both covered in water and not covered in water, so one of the two sense experiences of the same spot must have been illusory. In at least one instance your senses have deceived you. Countless other instances yield the same conclusion. Descartes' first point is merely a caution: our senses sometimes deceive us, he says, and we would be wise not to trust them completely even if they have deceived us only once. This ought to make us suspicious of Locke's hypothesis; sensations are not always caused by objects outside the mind that generally resemble the ideas based on those sensations. But to think the senses might *always* deceive us seems a bit too ridiculous to think about. It is admittedly far-fetched and ridiculous to raise practical or subjective doubts about the status of normal sense experience but for Descartes it is a philosophical necessity since he wants philosophical certainty about his most fundamental beliefs. He must therefore try to find some reason to doubt Locke's Hypothesis, given that it is the most basic of all his beliefs and the one in which nearly all his other beliefs are grounded.

Is it possible my senses always deceive me? Wouldn't I be mad to think this? At the level practical of subjective certainty the answer is yes. It would be a sign of mental illness to seriously think my senses might be deceiving me. But philosophically it's a different story. It may be impossible in principle to prove that I am not insane. If I cannot prove that I am not insane then my senses could always be deceiving me. I know of other people who are clearly insane and their senses are always deceiving *them*, even though they are subjectively certain that they are perfectly sane and that their sense experiences are *veridical* (true representations). They say they are flying when they are not. They say they are Christ or Napoleon or an orange when they are not. I knew one man who thought he was being attacked by bees when no bees were evident to anyone else in the room. How can I prove that I am not insane like him? If I can't, I cannot be metaphysically certain that my senses are not now deceiving me. I could be the victim of a consistent hallucination. And the more insane I am the more I am likely to protest that I am *not*.

Descartes does not quite draw the conclusion from the insanity possibility that he must be metaphysically uncertain about the status of his experiences. But unfortunately he has similar experiences rather often. He has little psychotic hallucinatory episodes every night when he dreams. In those episodes he believes on the basis of his sensory data that he is flying, or being chased by thieves, or making love to a beautiful woman, or drinking wine, or eating an apple. He could even be dreaming that he is sitting on a couch reading the introduction to a play called *Cartesian Dreams*. In fact I could be dreaming right now that I am at a desk writing about such a play. I won't believe it subjectively or practically, but can I be philosophically certain that I am not? Can you be philosophically certain that you are not now dreaming that you are seeing the word 'Cartesian' in front of you? Can you disprove beyond all possible doubt that you are not someone else of another gender and from another century dreaming that he or she is reading these words? Perhaps you should check your driver's license, smack your cheeks, look out your window, or phone a friend to prove you are not dreaming. But this won't work. If you are really dreaming then you would only be dreaming the license, the cheeks, the friend, and the window. You might try thinking "I remember dreaming last night then waking up this morning and not going back to sleep all day. So I must be awake now." However, if you are now dreaming then you are dreaming that you remember waking up, so that thought does not move you one centimeter closer to philosophical certainty about the status of your sense experiences. You might be dreaming you are awake.

You can't be philosophically certain that you are now wide awake and not dreaming so you can't be philosophically certain that you are having veridical perceptions of the real world. This is all Descartes wants to demonstrate with his dreaming argument. His point is that we must be speculatively distrustful of the senses and their evidence: we cannot rely on perceptual testimony as a foundational source of philosophical knowledge. Descartes has now cast doubt on both aspects of Locke's Hypothesis. First, our senses frequently mislead us about the way extra-mental reality really is. Often there is no resemblance between our ideas and the external objects that cause those ideas. Second, we cannot be certain that there is an external world *at all.* All our experiences could be psychotic or dream-induced delusions. Descartes goes on until he finds something underived from sense experience that he cannot theoretically doubt. I will return to his argument later.

For now, try to imagine what would happen if you lost your grip on the distinction between subjective or practical doubt and philosophical doubt. Then you would know what a Cartesian dream would be like. You wouldn't know the difference between thinking you might be dreaming and dreaming you might be thinking. This is what I imagine happened to Descartes during the three days of his death. He lost his mind in a fever and with it the clear distinction between philosophy and psychosis. Thanks to Queen Christina he came to his senses. She restored his practical and subjective certainties about sense experience while crucifying his ambitions for philosophical ones.

As a matter of historical fact Queen Christina of Sweden was a brilliant, highly educated, and eccentric monarch. She couldn't decide if she was gendered as a man or as a woman. Biologically she was a female with a misshapen body. She seems to have been thoroughly confused about love, sex, and marriage. She had a knack, however, for identifying gifted male thinkers in the arts and sciences. She corresponded with many of them and lured several European luminaries to her court in Stockholm. Descartes was one of them. He went to Sweden at Christina's request in the fall of 1649 on the assumption that he would be giving her tutorials in metaphysics. He told several of his friends he would die there, which he did.

When he reached Stockholm Descartes' assumption turned out to be wrong. The Queen instead requested that Descartes write the lyrics to a ballet she had composed. Descartes did so on the condition that the philosophy lessons would commence as soon as the lyrics were written. (I have read the lyrics and they are appallingly bad – a fact I ignore in the play.) When the lessons began Christina insisted they be on the subject of love rather than metaphysics. She had been captivated by Descartes' *Passions of the Soul.* Moreover, she demanded that Descartes give the lessons at five in the morning during Sweden's coldest winter in forty years. Clearly, the play opens with a series of conflicts. A man and a woman, each possessed of immense intellectual gifts and continental fame, cannot agree on anything. Their conflicts remain intensely passionate throughout most of the play until everyone realizes that

Descartes is dying from the severe pneumonia brought on by his walks from his lodgings to the castle in the frigid mornings. Up to this point the historical details in *Cartesian Dreams* are accurate, although they are staged in a sometimes clownish, surrealistic, dream-like way from the outset. Indeed, the entire play is someone else's dream of Descartes death. Beyond that I have fictionalized all the values and ideals compressed into the radically polarized characters of Descartes and Christina. After all, I'm reporting a dream. I still don't know if this play should be read as comedy or tragedy, or perhaps tragi-comedy.

Cartesian Dreams can be read from one point of view as a clash between Descartes' male European reason and Christina's passionate female corrective to it. Reason is put in its place but not *displaced* by the Queen's romanticism and sensualism. She exposes the inherent limitations and contradictions of reason, thereby dissolving the pretensions and misguided ambitions on which western philosophy has thrived since its inception. Descartes' moribund madness signifies the collapse of rationality, or perhaps the failure of philosophical modernity, and its transformation into sensualism and (significantly) into art. The Queen abdicates her throne to live an itinerant life as a dancer. Her servant leaves the castle to raise her child – fathered by Descartes' butler. The only one to persist in an attempt to complete Descartes' project is the young Princess Elizabeth of Bohemia who, in actual fact, was Descartes' scholarly protégé and with whom Descartes was undoubtedly in love. It was Princess Elizabeth, a woman, who first pointed out with incisive clarity the severity of Descartes' mind-body problem. Queen Christina, however, abandons philosophical reason, at least in my theatrical version of her. Notice she does not abandon Descartes himself. She rejects his philosophical ambitions and methods but she loves him.

Still, all this happens in a dream. It is a *Cartesian* dream. It is a dream in which reason dies and the last scene informs us that it is a dream everyone must repeat. Philosophy is absurd but nobody can do without it. We must all yield to its seductive and demonic call before we can transcend or abjure it. Martin Luther liked to say that Reason is a whore: after you've been to bed with Reason you must pay a price and you want her to leave. Three hundred and fifty years after Descartes we are still finding Reason's charms irresistible and we still pay the price. Three hundred and fifty years later, moreover, professional philosophers still devote their time and energy to the mind-body problem bequeathed by Descartes at the end of his *Meditations* to subsequent centuries. In fact the mind-body problem is one of the two or three most important problems in contemporary philosophy. An outline of the development of this problem in the *Meditations* should shed some light on important moments in *Cartesian Dreams*.

Recall how in the first section of the *Meditations* Descartes was trying to find a philosophical certainty resistant to all theoretical doubt. To do this he used doubt as his tool: he would subject the foundations of all his beliefs to a skeptical inquisition until he discovered something indubitable. Since what he had seen, heard, smelled, tasted, and felt provided the source of most of his beliefs he was compelled to ask if he could trust the deliverances of his senses. The dream argument "almost convinced" him that beliefs based on senses experiences were philosophically uncertain.

Descartes goes on to adduce even more subtle reasons for doubting all beliefs derived from sense experience. It is true of course that most beliefs are in fact derived from the testimony of our senses. The full title of Descartes' text, however, is *Meditations on First Philosophy in Which the Existence of God and the Real Distinction of the Soul and Body are Demonstrated*. Descartes wants to *prove* that God exists and that our mind (soul) and body can exist apart from each other. If they can't then the possibility of a disembodied immortal afterlife is dashed. Now, God and the mind are conceived of as immaterial entities. They are not extended objects in space; they do not have weight, length, breadth, or depth. Accordingly they do not have any empirical or sensible qualities, meaning they have no qualities perceivable by the senses such as color or odor. Therefore God and mental nature cannot be known or understood through the senses. That is why Descartes must get rid of sense experience as a basis for knowing and understanding the non-sensible nature of God and the mind. In philosophical language, Descartes must replace a theory of knowledge known as Empiricism with another one known as Rationalism.

Descartes makes his skepticism about sense experience complete with two very powerful arguments. The first one starts from the premise that there might be a God who is perfect in power, knowledge, and benevolence. If such a being exists, it would be inconsistent with that being's attributes to permit the senses to be deceived because deception is not benevolent. But the senses *are* deceived, sometimes dramatically. So if God exists He must be less than perfectly benevolent or less than perfectly powerful. It is conceivable that there is such a being and the less benevolent and the less powerful this being is the more likely it is that it would chronically deceive us.

The second argument is a knockout. It consists in the claim that there *could* be a perfectly evil and powerful being, a kind of cosmic hypnotist who has nothing better to do than deceive us at every instant of our lives. How likely it is that this evil genius exists is irrelevant. If such a being's existence is logically possible – and it is – then everything we mentally experience could be an illusion. Like a brain wired to a supercomputer which controls every input to produce hallucinations, our brains could be controlled by the evil genius such that every sense experience we have is illusory. And worse than

Meditation 2

that, given the supreme wickedness and power of this possible being, every mental event – not just sensations – could be false. Everything we think we remember could be false. Every emotion could be delusional. Every belief could be false. Every calculation in mathematics or logic could be mistaken. Every sense of subjective or practical certainty could be a cruel hoax. Indeed, I could be deceived about who I am. I could be someone else hallucinating that they are me.

Descartes really has us on the ropes here. There is no way to be philosophically certain that there is *not* an evil genius because every attempt to disprove its existence could be affected by the evil genius itself. Consequently, there is not one thing that is philosophically certain. Every mental event could be manipulated by the evil genius. But now something is certain, and it is philosophically certain. Someone, whoever it is, is having mental experiences – though they may all be deceptive – and these mental experiences are intimately present in the mind of what I now call 'me'. Whatever is directly aware of those experiences, the first-person bearer of them, cannot doubt their existence.

I think I feel a pain in my foot. The evil genius may be deceiving me about this. I may not have a foot at all. If my senses deceive me I may not even have a body. But I cannot doubt that I think I feel a pain in my foot. If I try to doubt that I am thinking I thereby prove that I am thinking. I cannot think that I am not thinking. Supposing ALL my mental experiences to be false or illusory, I cannot doubt that I am having them. If I doubt that I am thinking I must be thinking because doubting that I am thinking is thinking. Hence I exist as a thinking being. I cannot doubt this. To think that I do not exist as a thinking thing is to prove that I exist – if I am thinking that I do not exist I must first exist in order to have the thought that I do not exist. So even if I am deceived about everything else I cannot possibly be deceived about that.

It is the only thing I cannot doubt. I am philosophically certain of it. Insofar as I think, I exist. Sometimes the only thing people remember about the history of Philosophy is Descartes' Latin phrasing of his first philosophical certainty: *Cogito ergo sum.* I think, therefore I am.

The fact that I exist is not a particularly stunning discovery. What matters is that Descartes is philosophically certain of it. It is an incorrigible belief and immune to all doubt. In Descartes' words, it is known "clearly and distinctly". Nothing else should be believed unless it is known with equal clarity and distinctness. What matters just as much is that I exist *as a thinking thing*. All I know with philosophical certainty is that I think, that I am a mind. I cannot be philosophically certain that I have a body because a body is a sensed object and all objects of sense at this point could be deceptions. I can *think* I have a body with arms, legs, a brain, and so forth, but I could be mistaken. I can *think* there is an external world outside me or I can *think* that Locke's Hypothesis is true but I could be completely mistaken about those things. In brief, as long as it is possible that an evil genius exists it remains possible that everything I think (sense, remember, feel, etc.) is false.

Descartes now tries to prove that there is no evil genius. His strategy is simple: prove that God exists. If God exists and if God is perfectly good then he would not always deceive us. Why He would allow us to be occasionally deceived needs some explanation, but if we could be philosophically certain that God exists then we could be confident that Locke's Hypothesis is true and that we have a body to which our minds are somehow connected. How they are connected is Christina's worry and Descartes' embarrassment. I will get to this problem in a moment.

Descartes' first proof for God's existence must necessarily begin with some subjective thought because his thoughts are the only things whose existence is philosophically certain. He can't point to alleged facts in the external world – such as its organization or design or even existence – since he is not yet philosophically certain that there is an external world. He must therefore start reasoning from one of his own ideas. Descartes may not know how it got into his mind or if it stands for anything real outside his mind but he cannot deny that he has an idea of a perfect being. He has no idea of anything else so perfect. This idea is an idea of an infinitely perfect being. In a complicated argument Descartes reasons that his idea of an *infinitely* perfect being must have been originally caused by an actual being having as much perfection as the amount of perfection the idea contains. Descartes knows he is not a perfect being and he cannot think of anything else except God as a perfect being, so God must be the original cause of his idea. No imperfect being (including Descartes himself) could have caused such an idea of perfection.

In a second argument Descartes asks us to try to think of a perfect being lacking the property of existence. Trying to do so is like trying to think of a square without four sides. Similarly, if I try to think of a perfect being without including existence in the concept of perfection then I am not thinking of a perfect being. I can only think of a perfect being as existing. If God lacked the property of existence he would not be perfect. So to think of a perfect being which is imperfect is a contradiction. To remove the contradiction I am compelled to think of a perfect being as existing, hence God exists.

Descartes exists, God exists, and now the external world exists. We can be sure the external world exists because God is not a deceiver. Material objects have real existence independent of our awareness of them and our awareness of them in normal circumstances reveals what they are really like. Locke's Hypothesis is true.

Our bodies are one of the potentially infinite number of material things in the universe. Eventually our bodies will die, dissolve, and disperse. The atoms and electrons from which our bodies are composed will go somewhere else when we die and become part of some other material nature. Does this mean that our minds – like our material brains – will someday be dead and gone? Or can our minds go on thinking independently of our brains? The belief in a continuation of personal mental life without a living body is probably the most ancient metaphysical belief in human history. Billions of people have believed it and billions still do. The belief is in some ways incredible. Unless Descartes' argument in the concluding meditation is sound the belief is probably false. His argument is that we must be able to form a "clear and distinct" conception of a mind *without* a body. This is the "principal prerequisite" for any belief in personal immortality. It is also what gives Descartes – as well as Elizabeth and Christina – the problem of conceiving a mind *with* a body. The mind-body problem is Descartes' greatest legacy to modern philosophy. *Cartesian Dreams* can be read as a play on that problem alone.

Let us set up the problem as Descartes does. The starting point is to ask what is contained in the clear and distinct ideas of bodily substance (*res extensa*) and thinking substance (*res cogitans*). By 'clear' Descartes means 'lucid', 'essentially basic', or 'utterly simple'. A clear idea contains all and only those primary elements comprising a thing's essence. By 'distinct' he means 'containing only what is clear', 'unconfused with other ideas', or 'not overlapping with other ideas'. His reasoning is that when we have sharpened a clear and distinct idea of bodily substance ("corporeal nature") and another one of thinking substance ("mental nature") we will discover that mind and matter are metaphysically different substances, radically so, such that we can easily think of each of them existing without the other. Indeed Descartes thinks they can be thought of as such radically different categories of being that it will soon become impossible for him to explain how they can coexist.

Forming a clear and distinct idea of bodily substance is not difficult. The ring on my finger is as good an example as any. What is its essential nature? Well, I immediately realize that it is not the same color as when I bought it. Nor is it the same shape. So being gold or being circular is not essential to its nature. But then I realize that it must have *some* kind of color and be *some* kind of shape. Having a shape and having a color seem to be essential to its existence. Being shaped and being colored are two of its primary characteristics. The particular color and particular shape are secondary characteristics: the shape of my ring can change but its having *some* shape cannot.

Why must my ring always have a shape (and color, and smell, and weight, and tactile qualities, and audible qualities)? Because it is extended in space. My ring or any other material thing in the universe – including a single molecule – must have these sensible qualities because it is extended in space. This is the essential nature of any body. It is pure *quantity* in its barest essence, mathematically describable in terms of length, breadth, depth, area, volume, mass, temperature, and weight. And because it has these measurable qualities it has the other sensed qualities of color, taste, sound, tactility, and odor. I can change the ring's measurements by cutting it in half but it will still have the primary qualities that make the sensed qualities possible. That is, bodily substance is divisible. Extension and divisibility are two of Descartes' irreducible and essential features for material substance. A third feature is monumentally important. When I inspect the ring I do not have the slightest reason to attribute a mental life to it. The same goes for every other purely material object in the universe. On what basis would I say that it has an inner life, or subjectivity, or consciousness? None whatsoever. The more I consider it the more it seems philosophically certain that it is part of the essence of material things NOT to think. A pure body is just there, passively and inertly taking up space, completely determined by the laws of physics and chemistry.

What is contained in the clear and distinct idea of thinking substance? Forming such an idea is also not so terribly difficult if we use an example analogous to the ring. Let us analyze some particular mental entity, such as an idea. (The analysis will turn out the same way for any other mental entity, such as a desire, a calculation, a memory, or a sensation.) Right now I am having an idea of Descartes shivering at his fireplace after a snowball fight at the castle with Christina. What I notice first is that the idea in my mind is not constructed of physical objects. I do not have physical things in my head called Descartes, Christina, a fireplace, a castle, and snow. I cannot show you my idea of Descartes shivering at the fireplace in the same way I can show you my ring. It would be absurd to say that my idea of Descartes is as heavy as Descartes, that my idea of snow is as cold as snow, that my idea of Christina is as tall as Christina, and that my idea of the castle is the same color as the castle. In fact my idea has no sensible, quantifiable properties at all because it is *unextended.* It is not located or locatable anywhere in space. I can describe it to you but you can never see it, or taste it, and so forth. It is also *indivisible.* The material things (Christina, Descartes, the snow) are physically separate things and they can be divided off from each other. My idea of Descartes-shivering-at-the-fireplace-after-a-snowballfight-with-Christina is a single indivisible entity. I cannot divide this idea into equal parts. I must think it either as a unity of its various conceptual "pieces" or I cannot think it at all.

The fact that mental entities and events are unextended explains many unique features of thinking substance. Mental entities such as ideas and the mental substance that bears them do not exist publicly, because they are unextended with no sensible properties. They do not have third-person status; no one else except the mind that has them can be directly aware of their existence and their subjective quality. Mental events and entities have only first-person status. Philosophers of mind describe this status by saying that each mind has "privileged access" to its own mental states and occurrences but access to another's mental states and occurrences is forever barred. Because of this the 'qualia' of my mental states cannot be known to anyone else, meaning that the subjectively experienced character and *'raw feel'* of my mental occurrences are incontrovertibly private. I can never know what red looks like to you nor can you know what it looks like to me. Neither can I know what the internal phenomenal feel of a pain is like for you. I know only that what I subjectively experience in my consciousness is described as 'red' or 'painful' in a public language. The subjective quality of experience-of-redness and experience-of-pain, however, is known only to the subject having those experiences even though we use the same word to refer to what might be radically different internal experiences.

The upshot of this is that I can objectively observe your body-events but not your mind-events. I can look at, photograph, or otherwise objectively record the neuro-chemical events in your brain while you are having a pain but I can't look at the pain itself when you subjectively experience it. The brain-event is only objectively observable; the felt mind-event is only subjectively experienced. One event occurs in the metaphysical domain of corporeal nature; the other occurs in immaterial consciousness, in the domain of mental nature. Technically, these are ontologically distinct domains – two categories of being each of which has properties separate and distinct from the other. This is the thesis of substance dualism.

Human beings are composites of these two substances. We are a dualistic mixture of two kinds of being. We are minds and bodies at one and the same time. There is a universal belief that at some point our bodies will whither and die so that we will exist only as mental beings, but while we are in the world we exist dualistically. In addition, the two parts of our nature are in constant two-way causal interaction. This is the thesis of causal interactionism. The mind-body problem consists partly in giving a coherent account of how this interaction occurs. How do the mind and body "commingle" (to use Descartes' word)? Here is Descartes' answer.

Suppose I drop a brick on my toe. This will initiate a series of empirically observable events. With refined instruments I could watch the pain receptors in my toe send electro-chemical signals to a neighboring neuron. I could watch this neuron send a miniscule molecular packet of neurotransmitters across a synaptic gap to the next neuron and so on all the way up my leg, into my spinal cord, and into my brain. I could even watch specific neurons firing in my brain as it registers what happened to my toe. But how does the *physical* sequence transform or cross over into the *non-physical* mental experience of pain? How does the material process become conscious? How did the body cause an effect in the mind? Descartes says that in a small part of the brain (the pineal gland) the vibrations of the physical brain stimulate a "certain motion" in the non-physical mind. This is utterly mysterious and absurd but it is Descartes' attempt to solve the interaction problem. And I challenge any dualist to do any better.

Suppose I realize I am about to drop a brick and I quickly move my foot so my toe doesn't get hit. My brain sends a very rapid signal to the muscles in my leg and my leg moves out of the way of the brick. I can watch this entire process at a micro-level. One neuron fires in my brain, initiating a sequence of neuronal firings down through my spinal cord and into my leg. In this case a non-physical mental event (willing my leg to move) has caused a physical response (my leg moving). But what caused that first neuron to fire in my brain so the whole subsequent chain of firings occurred? Again, Descartes claims that a certain "mental excitation" in the pineal gland produced a signal in the brain to move my foot. Thinking substance somehow leapt over the metaphysical gap between itself and unthinking bodily substance and my foot moved.

Descartes account is incoherent for two reasons. First, he asserts that thinking substance is unextended and that extended substance does not think. But because thinking substance is unextended it would follow that it cannot be "contained in" anything, including the pineal gland. To be "within" something is to be in space, but minds are not in space by Descartes' definition. Hence they cannot in any way be "in" a pineal container nor in any other cortical container – no matter how big or how small. Second, physical events cause physical effects and mental events cause other mental effects. It is logically impossible under Descartes' account, however, for mental events to produce physical effects or for physical events to cause mental effects. This is because he claims that the ontological properties of minds and bodies are incompatibly contradictory. If they were not "really distinct" Descartes would have to concede that the mind dies with the body. Since he does not believe that happens he has to say that the mind has absolutely NO extended material properties. On that basis it can continue to exist in a *disembodied* state after the body disintegrates. He consequently made mind and body so incommensurably different that their mutual interaction is precluded. Nonetheless, they obviously interact. That is why Descartes' dualism account seems so absurd. But again, I do not think any substance dualist can do much better.

Descartes' framing of the mind-body problem makes it impossible to solve. He affirms the following two propositions :

> *(1) Mind and body are metaphysically distinct substances.*
> *(2) Mind and body causally interact.*

These propositions cannot both be true. (1) precludes (2) and (2) precludes (1). Since (2) seems so patently true and if (1) makes the truth of (2) impossible, most contemporary philosophers have concluded that (1) is false. Mental events are really no more than subtle and complex brain/nervous system events. The interaction problem is thereby dissolved. Sadly for Descartes so is the hope of immortality.

Queen Christina would by now have become quite impatient with all this, dismissing it as a species of very intelligent but eccentric silliness. At this point she would implore Descartes to "Stop thinking and start loving me!". She doesn't care if it's from the mind or the body as long as it is love-drenched sensuality. She knows Descartes is going insane as his fever heightens and she knows he cannot tell the difference between dreams and reality. For Descartes the hypothetical and theoretical doubts of the first meditation have become existentially and practically real. Detached deliberation has become bed-wetting panic. His only solace is the prospect of disembodied bliss in heaven. Christina, however, is a naturalist. Solutions, for her, have to be found within *this* world, since the naturalist posits no other. So she says to Descartes: "I don't care if you think you are dreaming or not, I'm going to teach you how to trust your senses and how to use them." And she does. She tries to show Descartes – the incarnation of moribund reason – that the mind and body can never be severed and that their happy commerce is more penile than pineal.

Or is disembodied immortality possible after all? Perhaps we would know if we could find out what Christina whispered to Descartes or what passed over the women after Descartes' death. But we don't know. That is why the dreamer of this play must retrace his (or her) dream all over again, awake with his own Christina or her own Descartes.

Reference: Feldman, F., A *Cartesian Introduction to Philosophy*. New York: McGraw-Hill, 1986.

CARTESIAN DREAMS

CAST OF CHARACTERS, IN ORDER OF APPEARANCE

CHRISTINA	Queen of Sweden
A SERVANT	The Queen's Lady-in-Waiting
HEINRICH SCHLUTER	Descartes' butler
RENE DESCARTES	French Philosopher
A DANCER	
ELIZABETH	Princess of Bohemia

All events take place at the Royal Palace in Stockholm from September 30th, 1649, to February 11th, 1650, and possibly at other times.

PROGRAM NOTE

Rene Descartes (1596-1650) is the founder of modern Philosophy. He unreservedly believed that the universe could be understood, and that foundational truths about it could be proven, by reason alone. His two most foundational certitudes – in his thought and his living – were God's existence and the radical separation of the mind and body. These two demonstrable truths, he thought, guarantee the possibility of immortal existence in the presence of Divinity.

He died from pneumonia, to which he fell ill in Sweden's winter while giving Philosophy lessons to the much younger Queen Christina. The lessons were given every morning at five o'clock. Descartes normally slept until noon.

Christina, Queen of Sweden, (1626-1689) ascended to her throne at age six and abdicated at age twenty-eight. Educated in the fashion of a male heir, she possessed a penetrating and encyclopaedic mind and was a major patron of the arts and sciences. In her youth she resolved never to marry, and never did. She invented a miniature brass cannon, now on display in a Stockholm museum, with which she shot fleas out of the air while reading philosophy in the nude.

SECOND PROGRAM NOTE

Article XC: That Which Springs From Delight

On the other hand, delight is especially instituted by nature to represent the enjoyment of that which gives pleasure as the greatest of all good things which pertain to man, which causes us to desire this enjoyment very ardently. It is true that there are various sorts of delight and that the desires which take their origin in these diverse varieties are not all equally powerful...The principal one is that which proceeds from the perfections which we imagine in a person whom we think may become another self; for with the difference of sex which nature had placed in men, as in the animals without reason, it has also placed certain impressions in the brain which it brings to pass that at a certain age, and in a certain time, they consider themselves defective, and as though they were but half of a whole, of which an individual of the other sex could be the other half. In this way the acquisition of this half is confusedly represented by nature as the greatest of all imaginable goods. And although we see many persons of this other sex, we do not for all that desire several at the same time, inasmuch as nature does not cause us to imagine that we have need of more than one half. But when we observe something in one which is more agreeable than what we at the same time observe in others, that determines the soul to feel only for the first all the inclination which nature gives it to seek for the good which that nature represents to it as the greatest that can be possessed; and this inclination or desire which thus springs from delight more usually receives the name of love than the passion of love, which has above also been described. It has likewise stranger effects and it is what provides the principal material for the writers of romance and for poets.

Descartes, *The Passions of the Soul*

ACT ONE

SET: The library-study in the royal castle. It is full of books, clutter, a
         telescope, a skeleton, and other anatomical debris. In one corner is a
         punching bag. The table is covered with letters, religious artifacts,
         and perfume bottles.

SCENE ONE

The house lights are on. Music up: Chopin, Sonata #2 in B-flat minor, 3rd
movement, at the end of the funeral march.

0:00-0:30   House lights on.

0:30-1:00   Slow fade to black.

1:00-1:25   Spotlight up slowly. The spotlight is on Christina's tiara, a large
              old book, a dumbbell, and a bottle of perfume.

1:30-2:00   Christina's hand enters the spotlight. It caresses the book and
              dumbbell. Christina sprays perfume on the other wrist.

2:00-3:57   Performance lights full. Christina does arm curls with the
              dumbbell, knee-bends, toe touching, etc., all in time to the
              music.

Christina: (Doing arm curls) Nulli est homini causa philosophandi, nisi
                   ut beatus sit. Cogito...Cogito. Sum...Sum. Cogito ergo sum.
                   (She then does ballet movements until the music ends. Enter
                   Servant at 3:30.) Is there any word from the ship?

Servant: Monsieur Descartes will be arriving soon, your majesty. A journey from Holland to Sweden would tax even the finest, yet he presses for an early audience.

Christina: Very well. I shall have him hear my Latin, so he thinks me to be a serious student of Philosophy.

Servant: Oh?

Christina: Yes. "Nulli est homini causa philosphandi nisi ut beatus sit".

Servant: What does that mean, your majesty?

Christina: "There is no reason to philosophize, except to have beatific bliss".

Servant: How excellently spoken.

Christina: An excellently spoken falsehood! My father educated me in Stoicism. For years I sought tranquillity in Philosophy and found none. Now I shall fertilise and comprehend my passions, which I have much forsaken. They are innocent, and instituted so by nature. They are the salt of life, which is insipid without them. That simple bliss so vaunted by philosophers is a tasteless state. Cogito. I think. Sum. I am. Cogito ergo sum. (At the punching bag) I think! I am! I am!

Servant: Your most serene majesty.

Christina: Yes?

Servant: Why do you, the Queen of Sweden, demand that he, a Frenchman, attend your court?

Christina: Because he is a philosopher, and has the greatest mind on earth. He is my apocalypse. He will instruct me where I am perturbed. I am febrile for truth.

Servant: And what does he reveal?

Christina: You may read it in here. (Hands the Servant a book.)

Servant: What is it?

Christina: His greatest work. Those are his demonstrations.

Servant: (Reading) "I have always thought that two questions, that of God that of soul, are chief amongst those that ought to be demonstrated by the aid of philosophy rather than theology. For although it suffices for believers like ourselves to believe by faith that the soul does not die with the body and that God exists, certainly no unbeliever seems capable of being persuaded of any religion or even any moral virtue, unless these two are first proven to him by natural reason".

Christina: God and immortality. Each may be a fact without the other. He sought to prove both.

Servant: Do you take each as proven your majesty?

Christina: (She turns downstage, sits. Takes a deck of cards from her underwear, turns, plays solitaire.) His words are a drunkard's nightmare…They crumble and dangle from his lips, unfermented in his juiceless logic. I heed them not. God is nothing if not love. To know of God, I must know of love. I would be rubbed by the thumb of love. Knowing love, I shall know eternity.

Servant: And love is unfamiliar with his logic.

Christina: God and the immortal soul are unfamiliar with his logic.

Servant:	Why then do you proceed with him?
Christina:	His brilliance is effulgent. He has written on the passions, their movements in the body and their affectations in the mind. His genius will aid me to express them.
Servant:	In the dance, your majesty?
Christina:	Yes, in the dance. He shall put the truth to music, and I shall make music into movement. (Knock at door)
Servant:	Who enters there?
Schluter:	(offstage) Your servant, Rene Descartes, announces his presence and respectfully seeks leave to introduce himself.
Christina:	But he was not summoned.
Servant:	(Through the door) The court is not prepared. Her majesty is indisposed. (Christina is playing solitaire.)
Schluter:	We would a word. The master is here. He has answers to her questions.
Servant:	What questions?
Christina:	I relayed to him three questions by the courier. Send in his answers.
Servant:	(Brings in a letter) To the first question: "What is the definition of love?" the philosopher replies: "Love is an emotion of the soul caused by the movement of the spirits which incites it to join itself willingly to objects which appear agreeable to it. And two sorts of love are usually distinguished, one of which is named the love of benevolence, that is to say,

the love which incites us to wish well what we love; the other is named the love of concupiscence, that is to say, the love that causes us to desire the thing that is loved. But it appears to me that this distinction concerns the effects of love alone, and not its essence; for as soon as we are willingly joined to some object, of whatever nature it may be, we have for it a feeling of benevolence, that is, we also join to it willingly the things we believed to be agreeable to it. (Christina yawns and fidgets.) This is one of the main effects of love. We also do not need to distinguish as many kinds of love as there are objects of it: The miser's love for money, ambition's love of glory, the drunkard's of wine, the brute's for a woman he violates, the honourable man's for a friend or mistress, all participate in love".

Christina: He is excessively verbose. Have him be succinct.

Servant: Her majesty says be succinct. (Schluter exits. Christina begins undressing. Schluter returns.)

Schluter: He will gladly be succinct.

Christina: Proceed with the second answer.

Servant: To the question "Will human understanding and inclination finally bring us to a love of God?" the philosopher replies: "Possible, but not likely."

Christina: Now he is too compact! The third question, "Which is worse? The excess and misuse of love, or of hate?"

Schluter: (Deadpan) Love.

Christina: Th-th-that is t-t-t-too su-su-succinct!

Schluter: (Confers offstage with Descartes, then returns.) Love is stronger than hate. Loving an unworthy object can make us worse than hating a loveable one. I ask you: Would you rather be associated with something bad or separated from something good?

Christina: (Now in leotards) Let Monsieur Descartes enter. He shall have an audience.

Descartes: (Enters) Your most serene majesty. I am at your pleasure.

Christina: At my WHAT?

Descartes: At your pleasure, your majesty.

Christina: And what is my pleasure, sir?

Descartes: I do not know, your highness.

Christina: And I do not know, Monsieur, how or in what sense you could then be said to be AT it. Perhaps you are at YOUR pleasure, and account mine at one with yours. Hence your thought is insidious or misguided. What would YOUR pleasure be, sir?

Descartes: Madame, my pleasure is what ought to be your pleasure: absorption in God and his promise of eternal life.

Christina: And that is what you are at, when you are at my pleasure? Do I mistake myself?

Descartes: Your majesty? Mistake your WHAT?

Christina: My self. I want to know if am I mistake my self.

Descartes: About what?

Christina: About my pleasure.

Descartes: The more assiduously I attend to your Queenship's words, the more readily I ascertain your need of my services. (The Servant and Schluter now begin to eye each other and fidget, edging towards each other.) I shall direct your attention to that Arcanum by which you are so distressed, I mean to say your inward self, and to its true constitution, which is so fitted by nature that it can both comprehend and comport with the pleasure it encounters therein and by which it is occasionally agitated. Hand me the second volume. (Schluter hands Descartes a book.) In this are contained the axioms and method by which we must be guided. I start with the principle which assumes reason to be…

Christina: Hold sir! Hold, I pray! (Crosses, takes book, reads). Monsieur Descartes, do you take to the dance?

Descartes: Your highness? I have seen the dance.

Christina: I would have you aid me in the dance. I have the music and the movements, but I have no words. I bid you write the words.

Descartes: With deepest respect, Madame, I am incredulous. I thought my station here to be that of instructor to your Queenship in matters metaphysical. You bade me advance your reason on the questions of God and the soul.

Christina: I did not! I wrote to you of love and other passions!

Descartes: And I have responded with my person, your majesty. I nonetheless propose for your royal consideration that a full comprehension of the passions is impossible unless it rests on the indubitable knowledge of the soul's true nature, and its kinship with the body. And this, I aver, demands knowledge of God and the universe he had furnished.

Christina: Am I to understand that the demonstrations of philosophy logically precede the expression and exercise of love?

Descartes: That is so, your majesty. Will and feeling must be shaped and guided by right reason and the truth it demonstrates (He puts down the book.)

Christina: (Looks puzzled. Paces.) This offends me! (Explosively) This was not your mission! This is duplicity!

Descartes: I disavow duplicity, your highness. I shall surely instruct you in the passions, but we are bound to follow the right course of reason and nature, putting the foundational principles of understanding before those derived from them. You have read my treatise on the first philosophy and you have read my treatise on the passions, and this permits me to remind you how the order of investigation should proceed. I shall instruct you first in metaphysics, so that our inquiries into the passions will rest on a firm and lasting foundation.

Christina: And should I become well versed in your demonstrations? Will you then assure me clarity in my passions?

Descartes: By the light of the noon-day sun, I swear it.

Christina: I see. I see. Nulli est homini causa philosophandi, nisi ut beautus sit.

Descartes: Madame?

Christina: Bliss will follow philosophy.

Descartes: Well spoken, your majesty. I am at your service.

Christina: The arrangements are made. You are to write four verses for the dance. Bring them here tomorrow, at four thirty in the morning, and we shall then commence the lessons according to your style. That is all.

Descartes: Your most venerable highness, I beg your leave to advance the hour. It is not my custom to...to be...

Servant: Her majesty is adamant, Monsieur, and her staff is more than firm. (Full exit by Christina and Servant)

Descartes: I see.

Schluter: Will you countenance her wishes?

Descartes: I will, good man. Yet I am struck incredulous that I acquiesce. She mentioned nothing of the dance, and more, she mentioned nothing of the hour, and even more, she mentioned nothing of the topic, prior to our setting out from Holland.

Schluter: Yet your marvellous reason prevails, sir. It shall be metaphysics before the passions.

Descartes: And do you not think, faithful sir, that it should be so? I shall explain. (Sits) We are stricken with awe that things exist, and what they do in their times and in their places. This giant wonder is the first of all that moves us, and has no opposite. It makes us marvel at the immense heavens, at the dancing flower drones, at music, at movements in the heart, at our hunger for eternity. It leads us to our feeble end, and hence to our pursuits and occupations in these strangest of times. It brings us to ourselves. (Schluter starts getting drowsy. Descartes speaks more to himself.) In ourselves we find dread and a delight in being, and this compels us to philosophy, wherein we lust for truth. Once in love with truth, and the immovable certitude it brings, we are tied in all the lover's knots and webs…we sometimes sigh…we sometimes grieve…we sometimes leap with hope…we sometimes sleep in turpitude and madness…(More loudly)…we often stand, our eyes transfixed in terror, the screams erupting from our bowels, "How did this begin?" "Why must it all end?" "What do you want me to do? (Louder) "Please! Please! Give me truth! I am in love with truth!" (Descartes looks sadly at Schluter, who is now asleep, and gently arranges his hair. He holds his hand. He whispers.) Our souls crave truth more than our lungs crave air. And what we find, we share. Her highness wants truth. And so, this day passed, I shall awake to the real work of a human being. I shall lead her to the starting point of certainty, and, by my method, to the truth she aches to know.

(Lights to black)

SCENE TWO

Music up:	Jean Phillip Rameau, Gavotte and six doubles, double #6, 1:03
Christina:	One, two, three and four. Bend, and pliè (lights up). (The Dancer is scantily dressed. She performs ballet movements. Christina is also scantily dressed in a leotard and is wearing a tiara. She periodically adjusts the dancer's movements. Music ends.) The dance must flow like lazy honey.
Dancer:	But it is so early. And we have danced since the mid of night.
Christina:	Pay it no mind. The lyrics will be here soon. For now, movement is our only certainty. (Knock at the door. Dancer sits obscenely. Throughout the scene she occasionally fondles her breasts.)
Schluter:	(Offstage) Monsieur Descartes announces his arrival. He has prepared the words and seeks to commence your lessons.
Christina:	Give him leave to enter (Descartes and Schluter stumble in, groggy, rubbing their eyes. Descartes hands Christina a sheet. She reads, hums, pirouettes, hands sheet back to Schluter.) They want revision.
Descartes:	Your highness, I am anxious to proceed. Let us begin. (Exit Schluter)
Christina:	Yes. Let us not be idle in our pursuit of metaphysics. Let it be done with so we may advance to love.
Descartes:	In good time. Our beginning will cultivate our outcome, and

contain it, and hence we must set out with utmost care and caution from a point of certainty. Not all beginnings will suffice.

Christina: Sir, I already do not follow you. I would rather you recapitulate your conclusions only. (She sprays perfume on her wrists.)

Descartes: No, Madame, by no means no. We must move from certainty to certainty by a proper method, to reach a certain end. We shall recognise the destination only through the process of arriving. Allow this point in your own manner. Tell me, what is the last pose and final chord in your ballet?

Christina: (Lies on floor in a death pose. Sings a minor chord) La-la-la-laaa-la-laaah.

Descartes: I put it to you that no mind can discern the import of this pose and chord, of this conclusion, without thorough knowledge of its origins and unfoldings. Do you not agree? (She nods.) My philosophy is no different. You must follow me. The truth is clearest in its seeking.

Christina: I reluctantly defer. What is your beginning?

Descartes: We must search for our first certainty.

Christina: Love is the only certainty.

Descartes: Not for the loveless. Not for the love-scorched. And love is not a proposition. It predicates and judges nothing.

Christina: So broken hearts and broken hopes are the only certainties.

Descartes: No, Madame. We are already off the subject.

Christina: Are you certain?

Descartes: I am certain.

Christina: You startle me with your brilliance, Monsieur. In less than thirty seconds you have found a certainty and we may begin. (She hugs him briefly and awkwardly.)

Descartes: Madame?

Christina: You are certain you have changed the subject.

Descartes: Which subject?

Christina: I am not myself certain. Only you are. (He looks puzzled, reflective. She hums a few bars of the Chopin Sonata and lifts the dumbbell.) Cogito ergo sum.

Descartes: I beg your pardon, your majesty, but we really have not begun.

Christina: (Doing knee-bends) We are all beginners. We are always beginning.

Descartes: Your royal highness. Let us go to the text. (He hands her one volume and reads from the other.) Page eight, your majesty, page eight. "It is now some years since I detected how many were the false beliefs that I had from my earliest youth admitted as true, and how doubtful was everything I had since constructed on this basis." (She is chewing her nails, fidgeting. He gestures to her and points to her book.) Please.

Christina: Please?

Descartes: Yes, please.

Christina: Yes please, what?

Descartes: Please read.

Christina: Certainly.

Descartes: Thank you.

Christina: You are most welcome. You are most abundantly welcome.

Descartes: For what?

Christina: You are just welcome. (Reads) "I was convinced that I must once and for all seriously undertake to rid myself of all the opinions which I had formerly accepted, and build a *new foundation*....

Descartes: (Dialogue overlaps on all italic type)...*new foundation*. Now I have delivered my mind from every care, and am happily agitated by no passions, I shall seriously and freely address myself to the general destruction of all my *former opinions*...

Christina: ...*former opinions*. Inasmuch as reason already persuades me that I ought to no less carefully withhold my assent from matters which are not entirely certain and indubitable than from those which are *manifestly false*... (pace quickens)

Descartes: ...*manifestly false,* if I am to find in each one some reason to doubt, this will suffice to justify my rejecting the whole. I shall only in the first place *attack those principles*...

Christina: ...*attack those principles* upon which my former opinions rested. (They gaze deeply at each other. They approach each other slowly.) I have always accepted as most true and certain what I have learned either from *or through the senses...*

Descartes: *...or through the senses,* but it is sometimes proved to me that these senses are sometimes deceptive, and it is wiser not to trust entirely to anything by which *we have once been deceived...*

Christina: *...we have once been deceived.* (They both gasp. They draw closer. Christina does some very slow dance movements. The Dancer also moves slowly. Christina speaks almost erotically.) Have your senses ever deceived you?

Descartes: (Gently) Most assuredly.

Christina: Do they deceive you now?

Descartes: It is a distinct possibility. I cannot prove they don't. So I must ingenuously cast into doubt all their deliverances, as you must.

Christina: Why, Monsieur?

Descartes: Doing so will deliver us from all possibility of error and falsehood.

Christina: My senses do not lie.

Descartes: How do you know? It is possible to doubt them. You may be insane. You may be someone else having delusions of being here, in Sweden, having fantastical conversations with another product of your demented delusions. How can you disprove it? Isn't it possible to doubt that this body and these hands are yours, that you are devoid of sense? Is it not possible that you are now dreaming? Is it not possible that your brain is so troubled by some effective potion taken in your food that nothing you now sense is real? Is this not a dream? You cannot disprove it.

Christina: Monsieur, you frighten me!

Descartes: Do not take to fright. Even if we are dreaming, it is not the stuff of nightmares.

Christina: Are we dreaming?

Descartes: We do not know. So we must hold the senses in doubt.

Christina: Is THIS a dream? (Christina points to the Dancer. Music up. Rameau, Gavotte, double #3,1:50. Descartes becomes enchanted. The Dancer does several dance movements, concluding her dance with her back to Descartes, staring at him with her head up between her legs, sticking her tongue out as the music ends.)

Descartes: We begin in doubt. We end in doubt.

Christina: Sir, you want a certitude immune to even the possibility of doubt. Any judgement susceptible to even the slightest of doubts you will not assent to. Such an expurgation! By eliminating the doubtful, you eliminate all possible false belief. Hence, you will doubt everything until you find a proposition which withstands all doubt, and you shall have unearthed your certitude. Have I understood you sir? Is doubt the sceptic's path to certainty?

Descartes: You are astute, your majesty. You learn quickly.

Christina:	And further, sir, do you doubt ALL the testimony of your senses because you cannot disprove the possibility that you may be insane? Or that you may be dreaming ?
Descartes:	That is it.
Christina:	And so you may say: (reads) "All these particulars, for example, that we open our eyes, shake our head, extend our hands, and so on, are but false delusions; and let us reflect that possibly neither our hands nor our whole body are such as they appear to be" (closes book). And you would add that perhaps nothing you now sense is as it appears to be.
Descartes:	That is my argument.
Christina:	(Sits, spreads her legs invitingly. Gestures to the Dancer, who positions herself close to Descartes, her face between her legs, almost in line with Descartes' crotch.) Are you now insane? Are you now dreaming?
Descartes:	I...I...am not...I am not certain. It is logically possible.
Christina:	Monsieur, if it is logically possible that your senses now mislead you, then I must ask what your experiences are like when it is logically possible that your senses do not deceive you. Would they be like this?
Descartes:	I am at a loss. I do not think so. I...I...am quite lost. We have gone far enough. The argument is clear.
Christina:	You teach quickly. But we cannot stop here. It chills me that it is not just possible that you are insane or dreaming but that it is likely. This prospect must surely bother me because I would

perforce account myself in the identical dilemma. Would it dispel your doubt, Monsieur Descartes, if I were to prove that you are now intact and awake?

Descartes: I should then be constrained to produce another argument.

Christina: And what might that be sir? (Dancer sits)

Descartes: (Reads) "I shall then suppose that some evil genius, no less powerful than deceitful, has employed his whole energy in deceiving me; I shall consider that the heavens, the earth, colours, figures, sound, and all other external things are nought but the illusions and dreams of which this genius has availed himself in order to lay traps for my credulity. I shall consider myself as having no hands, no eyes, no flesh, no blood, nor any senses, yet falsely believing myself to possess all these things. I shall remain obstinately attached to this idea, and if by this means it is not in my power to arrive at the knowledge of any truth, I may at least with firm purpose avoid giving credence to any false thing, or bring imposed upon by this arch-deceiver".

Christina: Smell this perfume.

Descartes: It is the dream.

Christina: Touch this hand.

Descartes: I am dreaming.

Christina: Hear my words.

Descartes: They are deceptions.

Christina: See my hair.

Descartes: It is all artifice. Some mind conspires against me.

Christina: Taste my lips.

Descartes: They are such…they are…I insist they are agreeable illusions.

Christina: Follow my movement.

Descartes: Nothing is certain. All is in doubt. Nothing is known.

(Music up, Chopin. Christina and Dancer dance slowly. Lights to black.)

SCENE THREE

Christina is playing solitaire. She is dressed regally in a full white gown, resembling a wedding gown. Knock at door.

Christina: If you have the words, enter.

Descartes: I have them. Now let us commence.

Christina: The words, let me see the words. (She reads from the sheet intently, humming periodically, gasping and sometimes moaning.) My dear man, you need write no more. There is no more to be written.

Descartes: Let us proceed, then. There is much to do. But I beg to tell you first that the hour is very early for one accustomed to lying abed until noon. The day is barely started. And the winter air here is cold enough to freeze my thoughts as much as it does the water. I fear I am taking on a chill. Would your highness postpone the lessons until the sun is higher?

Christina: It cannot be done. This is my royal stand. My hunting lessons begin with breakfast.

Descartes: Very well, your majesty. Let us review our progress.

Christina: I have thought of you, and your doubts.

Descartes: What were those doubts?

Christina: That all deliverances of the senses may be false. That all belief is uncertain.

Descartes: Very good. Why?

Christina: Because it is impossible to prove that we are sane. Because it is impossible to prove that we are not dreaming. Because there may be some abominable intelligence which perpetually deceives us.

Descartes: So nothing is certain and beyond doubt.

Christina: Nothing except that. And the fact that you said it to me.

Descartes: Even that your highness, is uncertain. Do you know, without the slightest shred of doubt, that I was here yesterday?

Christina: Of that I am certain.

Descartes: But, your majesty, it was only a dream. Or it was possibly a dream. Of that I am certain.

Christina: No, it was not a dream. Or am I dreaming now?

Descartes: It is possible that you are. But even if you are not, it is beyond question that you have no means for comparing what you now think you remember with the actual events of which those memories are the purported records. Are dreams and memories the residues of anything at all?

Christina: Monsieur Descartes, I begin to feel again that I am in a whirlpool, all of your making.

Descartes: But we must go on, even if our senses and our memories cannot be trusted. We must go on from here. (Points to book, from which she reads.)

Christina: "I suppose, then that all the things I see are false; I persuade myself that nothing has ever existed of all that my fallacious memory represents to me. I consider that I possess no senses; I imagine that body, figure, extension, movement and place are but fictions of my mind". (Christina now begins to feel her face, arms, legs. Does the same to him). "What then, can be esteemed as true? Perhaps nothing at all, unless there is nothing in the world that is certain".

Descartes: So you are certain of nothing?

Christina: I am uncertain even that it is I who bears uncertainty. I AM UNCERTAIN THAT I EXIST!

Descartes: Your majesty, were this were not philosophy, I would think you unbalanced in entertaining such thoughts (chuckles).

Christina: (Explosively) My good and esteemed man! You murder my thoughts! I have strayed through my castle most of the ghastly night, in a nightmarish dread that your sceptical questions have dissolved me and all that I behold. I cannot so much as affirm my own existence! (With increasing intensity and volume) Whose heart beats here? What walls are these? Where is yesterday? Who am I, if I am anything?

Descartes: Gently, gently, Madame. Those are only thoughts.

Christina: (Angrily) But they undo me! They dissolve me! They dissemble my world!

Descartes: Madame, observe. (He hurriedly picks up some available props, including some fruit, a large feather, her jewels, the dumbbell, books, some of her clothing, a picture of a baby, a wig, the tiara, and an enema bag. He puts them all on the bed and covers them with a blanket). This bed is your mind. Everything under the blanket is a thought in your mind.

Christina: My bed is my mind?

Descartes: It's only an illustration. Now, follow my reasoning. These are all mental contents. Let us say that this is a desire. (He holds up the baby picture.) And this is a memory. (He holds up the apple.) And this is a fear. (He points to the skeleton.) And this is love. (He holds up the enema bag.) All these things are in your mind only and they are all in doubt. You do not know if your desire is real; it is possible that your desire is fear. You do not know if your memory is accurate. Your pleasure might really be disguised pain. Do you follow?

Christina: And my love?

Descartes: Your gracious majesty! You refer to me as your love?

Christina: What of the mental experience we call love?

Descartes: No-one is certain what love is. And what you think your experience of love is may in fact be something quite different. Fear, for example...or lust...or the echoes of solitude...Hmmm...so it must also be doubted. All you know is that you are having a mental experience.

Christina: (Dejected) I follow you sir. My love may be no more than hope in disguise.

Descartes: Excellent. Now let us examine another class of mental experiences (holds up a book). We will call them beliefs. Unlike feelings or choices, these beliefs put forward a statement or claim that such-and-such is true. Can you think of any examples?

Christina: The world is round. God exists. The soul is immortal. Twice two is four. Water freezes. My breasts can make milk. When I was thirteen...the movement...music was in my hips and something filled up my breasts...the water...I...I...

Descartes: That is adequate. Now let me ask you, is it not possible that all these beliefs are false?

Christina: Yes, it is possible.

Descartes: Why?

Christina: Because they may be, every one of them, the product of a malignant madness. Because they may all be implanted by a demented genius or some alien mind which sports with us. Because this may all be a dream.

Descartes: My dear, majestic, royal woman! My most esteemed Christina! I am ecstatic! You comprehend the argument! You advance so rapidly! I embrace you! (He hugs her. They gaze at each other and fondle each other's hands.)

Christina: You are not there. Your ecstasy is wispy and insubstantial. It is not real.

Descartes: I shall pretend this is real.

Christina: Can you be certain that you are really pretending? And can I be certain that I am seriously and actually pretending that you are really there? (She touches his face. She fondles her breasts.)

Descartes:	The problems are legion.
Christina:	Monsieur Descartes, we are set loose in each other's dreams.
Descartes:	Let us proceed. We must find a nugget of certainty in all this. Have you read the entire treatise?
Christina:	I have. Truth and certainty are arriving. May I summarise? (He nods rapturously.) The bed is my mind. On the bed are all my mental contents. Of each and every one of them none may be taken as accurate or true. No belief is certain. I transfer this reasoning to my own mind. I survey all that I believe, all that I hold true, all my mental contents, and I conclude that every belief I cherish, or come to cherish, may be false.
Descartes:	Yes! Yes! And what then?
Christina:	And then I realise that it is ME, MYSELF, CHRISTINA, who may be mistaken. It is my dream, my delusion, my deception. I am only my thought and my experiences. But even if they all issue from deception and illusion, even if they are all false, they are MINE! They are my thoughts, and I must exist in order to have them. I am, I exist, because I think.
Descartes:	Yes, your majesty, you exist as a thinking being, even though all your thoughts may be false. Can you doubt that?
Christina:	No, Rene, I cannot. For I must exist in order to doubt.
Descartes:	I adore your perspicuity. You have found the bedrock of certainty. Your knowledge is clear and distinct. You clearly and distinctly perceive the truth of "Cogito ergo sum". So let us henceforth admit as true and certain all that you perceive with equal clarity and distinctness.

Christina: And if there is nothing?

Descartes: Then we shall remain bounded in our private, drifting dreams.

Christina: But for now we have won the day. I clearly and distinctly know that I exist as a thinking human being. Cogito! (Hits bag) I think! Sum! (Hits bag) I am. Cogito ergo sum!

Descartes: I think! (Hits bag) I think therefore I am! (Hits bag. Descartes and Christina do a jig together)

Together: Cogito! I think. I exist. I know I exist. Sum. We think, therefore we are… (Lights to black).

SCENE FOUR

(All players are on-stage. The dancer is doing burlesque moves. Schluter and the Servant are tickling each other and flirting. Descartes is adrift in thought. Christina is pacing in a two-piece bikini, ballet shoes, and tiara)

Christina: Are you thinking?

Servant: No, we never think.

Schluter: I am not thinking.

Christina: What are you doing?

Schluter: We are feeling.

Christina: Perhaps you think you are feeling.

Descartes: Feeling is a species of thought. A feeling is in the mind, and the sole essence of the mind is thought, therefore feeling is a form of thought.

Schluter: Now I feel I am thinking.

Servant: Do you feel what you think?

Schluter: I think I feel.

Servant: I sense you are thinking now.

Schluter: I feel you sensing my thoughts.

Christina: Do you think your senses are working?

Servant: I feel they are.

Schluter: I sense that I am feeling now. (Bends down to look closely at the dancer.) No, I feel that I am sensing. (He fondles the dancer, the Servant slaps his hand and straddles him on the floor.)

Christina: I think I would rather feel. I feel that I would rather think. Is there sense in all this? Do you remember the last feeling you had?

Servant: It was this. (She is rocking on Schluter.)

Christina: How do you know that? How can you be certain?

Servant: I do not need certainty. Certainty ruins pleasure.

Christina: That thought is possibly true. I do not think that, nor do I sense that, nor do I feel that. (She helps the dancer to her feet.) I remember that.

Descartes: Expel these concupiscent mammals, with their disordered prattle. They profit from nothing. Christina, we must turn to Philosophy.

Christina: You are all dismissed. (They all exit.)

Descartes: Excuse my abruptness, your highness. I fear I am in the grip of a fever. The wintry walk from my lodgings to your castle is exciting my lungs.

Christina: It will pass, Monsieur. Let us put philosophy before us. I am vexed after yesterday's argument.

Descartes: Please expound your vexation.

Christina: You have demonstrated that the only thing of which I can absolutely and incorrigibly certain is my mental existence.

Descartes: That is so.

Christina: And further that it is possible that everything I think and everything I sense is a deception.

Descartes: Yes, Christina.

Christina: Consequently, the only certitude is my existence and my private thoughts. (He nods.) Then my vexation is this: How will I ever come to know that there is a world outside my thoughts, that consciousness exists in other beings, that I have a body, with real sounds and sights and fluids...with a heart that beats...and hair...and hands in my hair, tumbling, romping...soothing hands...

Descartes: You want to know beyond all doubt that you are not alone, that you are not the only inmate of solitary confinement. (She nods sadly.) We will find a way. The jungle of subjectivity lets in light. It lets in moisture, it must! My tears must be true moisture. My breath must be true air. I cannot be alone! I must get out of my mind!

Christina: You can.

Descartes: How? How?

Christina: Love will do it. Try love.

Descartes: No, no, Christina, love is the greatest deception of all. We must proceed from one clear and distinct idea to another.

Christina: God is love. Are you deceived about that? (She removes her tiara. He looks puzzled. He paces. She hums Chopin, picks up the dumbbells, does knee-bends, moans with pleasure.) You want to reason your way through this forest of doubt.

(Descartes picks up the treatise, mumbles to himself.) This labyrinth of mystery.

Descartes: Mmmm…this labyrinth. There is a route.

Christina: This prison of despair. (Descartes furiously leafs through the book.) This coffin of lovelessness. (Christina now awkwardly tires to put her feet behind her head.) This desert of reason. (She falls over, sprawled on her back.) Have we failed?

Descartes: We have not. We cannot. The argument has not begun.

Christina: Nothing has begun.

Descartes: But we exist! We know we think!

Christina: But thought itself may be disordered. We may yet be dreaming. The evil genius may be toying with our minds. In our dreams and deception, Rene, we may esteem ourselves certain of some few things, and that certainty itself may be a cruel illusion. (She tries to stand on her head.)

Descartes: So we must reason as follows. We must prove we have clear and distinct knowledge that an almighty God exists, that he is perfect and therefore no deceiver, that he is the source of truth and certainty, that he remains an eternal companion, that he created our indivisible souls…without parts and pieces…timeless rest…comfort us and give us succour…a place in heaven…quiet as the stars…a love so firm…so lasting…so exquisite and sublime…the smooth, soothing hands of divinity…a womb without weight…I…I

Christina: Descartes. (He slowly approaches her, looking longingly into her eyes.) Rene. (She slowly removes his jacket while speaking.) You ache for God and a home in paradise.

Descartes: You ache too, Christina.

Christina: We both ache. We will go on aching. There is no way out. You are alone and aching. You can prove nothing beyond that. You have given yourself only one escape, and that is reason. Why do you put your faith in reason? Will it get you out of this? How can you trust it? If you are going to doubt everything, that is the first thing you should doubt.

Descartes: I trust it because God gave it to me, and he gave me a method for using it.

Christina: But every belief is still in doubt, including that one. In your dreams or in your madness, or in your delusions forged by a monstrous prankster, you may be tragically wrong in your reliance on reason. Every inference, every deduction, every premise may be a chimera, a baseless step. You have barred yourself forever from further thinking. You cannot use reason to prove the claims of God and immortality, because reason itself in under your microscope of doubt. You are sinking, and time is short. (She unbuttons his shirt.)

Descartes: Adrift without an anchor. Lost in the fog. A moon without a planet.

Christina: Yes, drifting, ungrounded. This may all be a dream. Layers upon layers of dreams, delusions, deceptions, misty flimsy vapours... fruitless prayers... pleading supplications... asking... wishing... aching...

Descartes: And yet…

Christina: And yet?

Descartes: And yet I might dream something true.

Christina: But you would never know it.

Descartes: I would! If it were a clear and distinct perception it would be true.

Christina: There aren't any. Name one.

Descartes: (Reads through the treatise.) Here. "I have in me then the idea of God, concerning which we must consider whether it is something which cannot have proceeded from myself. By the name of God I understand a substance that is infinite, eternal, immutable, independent, all-knowing, all-powerful, and by which I myself and everything else, if anything else does exist, have been created. Now all these characteristics are such that the more diligently I attend to them, the less do they appear capable of proceeding from me alone; hence we must conclude that God necessarily exists. For although the idea of substance is within me owing to the fact that I am substance, nevertheless I should not have the idea of an infinite substance – since I am not infinite – if it had not proceeded from some substance veritably infinite." (He beams triumphantly.) You see? Only God could give rise to my idea of him. I know that clearly and distinctly.

Christina: It is neither clear nor distinct to me.

Descartes: Then your reason is deficient.

Christina: (Angrily, explosively) MY reason! YOUR errors are transparent. Rene Descartes, devoted to truth, clarity, coherence, rigid consistency, you – a paradigm of rationality – and you do not see that simplest of mistakes, You foolish simpleton! Your genius betrays you. You have no guarantee that your idea of God is adequate or correct. You may be insane. You MAY BE DREAMING! The arch-deceiver may be fooling you. Even supposing your idea of God to be correct and adequate, it is madness to think that only God could cause it…more likely, it is the product of dreams and afflictions, or else a demented sadist has lodged it in your thoughts. You are lost. You are lashed forever on a rack of doubt. Your doubt has defeated you!

Descartes: (Descartes begins to sob quietly, then breaks into uncontrollable crying. Christina punches the bag, then skips a rope while he cries.) NO! My argument fails only because I am infirm. My mind, my instrument, is not operating efficiently. It cannot end here! We must begin again! (Descartes sobs, Christina skips her rope and hums.)

Christina: Give it up Rene. You have tried to use doubt to reach certainty. But it got you even deeper into the quagmire of suspicion. Now you have the despair of solipsism.

Descartes: Do you know exactly what that means? Solipsism?

Christina: I know exactly what it means. I have known it for years. You gave me the word for it. As an idea it is interesting…that one cannot prove beyond any doubt that there is anything at all outside one's own mind…that I am the only mind in the universe…it is fascinating. But to live and breathe the pulsing truth of solipsism is purgatory. It is my worst nightmare. It terrorises me. There is no exit from such a hellish void.

Descartes: Christina, do not leave me to brood in it.

Christina: How can I leave you? If the idea is true, I do not even exist for you… I am in your mind only. (She exits.)

Descartes: I am in hell. Are these my hands? (He looks at his hands, exploring them, and begins to shiver.) It is the illness. It is advancing rapidly. Reason is gone. Soon I will be gone. I know nothing. (He feebly punches the bag.) Cogito. Sum. I think I am. Is that all? Is that the end of my thinking? (Sobs) I am a monk without a prayer. (Enter Schluter)

Schluter: Sir, are you unwell? Her Royal Highness expresses concern.

Descartes: Are you really there? Am I dreaming?

Schluter: Good sir, you must soon repair to bed.

Descartes: Am I dreaming that I am awake? Is my memory of sleeping last night part of today's dream?

Schluter: Master, I will prepare your room.

Descartes: Schluter, is that you? Could I really be someone else? Is there anyone else? Does anything exist? Oh God, if there is one, save my soul, if I have one.

Schluter: I will return quickly. (Exits)

Descartes: I am not clear. I am not even distinct. I ache. I am tired. I must sleep, or I must dream that I am sleeping…in my dreams the thread of clarity will knit itself… to sleep, if only to sleep…an illuminating darkness… a moment's freedom from this cage… this necessary solitude… my hermitage of doubt… (He sobs, and starts shivering again. Lights to black.)

ACT TWO

SET: A sparsely and delicately furnished bedroom, wispy and feminine. A lavish bed and night table. A skeleton.

SCENE ONE

(Christina is reading the treatise. She is wearing only her bikini and tiara. The dancer is sitting on the floor with her ankles behind her neck. Schluter enters.)

Schluter: Your majesty, Monsieur Descartes asks that the lesson be abandoned this morning. His illness seems more grave.

Christina: She is stuck. Help her please. (Schluter tries unsuccessfully to unlock the dancer's ankles. After much commotion he finally gives up with exhaustion. She then undoes herself and exits giggling.) You say his condition has worsened?

Schluter: It has, Madame. He had to remain in the castle overnight.

Christina: I see. Please go and summon him. Tell him I fathom his despair and that I can relieve it. Go quickly. (He exits. She reads.) "Philosophy signifies the study of wisdom, and by wisdom is meant not only prudence in one's affairs, but a perfect knowledge of everything which man can know, as much as for the way he conducts his life as for the preservation of his health and the invention of all the arts and sciences. Living without philosophy is like keeping ones eyes shut without ever trying to open them, and the pleasure of seeing all the things which our vision discloses cannot be compared to the satisfaction found through the knowledge philosophy gives. This study is more necessary for the study of our lives than is the use of our eyes in guiding our steps". (She closes the book.) Nisi us beatus sit...(Descartes enters, wrapped in a blanket.)

Descartes: I perspire. There is a fever in my head.

Christina: We shall terminate the lessons. Your scepticism is an arid wasteland. I want to study the passions.

Descartes: Christina?

Christina: Yes?

Descartes: The purpose of philosophy is the acquisition and expression of foundational truth. The possession of this truth is an unconditional necessity for living well and dying well. I told you several days ago that knowing of God and the soul's relation to the body is requisite for the regulation and prosecution of our lives. Reason and understanding must go before choice and feeling. I am sorrowful that my proofs for divinity fail me. But I have put my mind through a burning trial throughout this terrible night, and I have the answers. Allow me to expound on them and our knowledge of the passions will easily follow.

Christina: Answers to what?

Descartes: Answers to questions of the soul, and its eternal essence, and its relation to the body.

Christina: Rene, you are wasting your time.

Descartes: Give me leave to try. I will not waste time.

Christina: Proceed.

Descartes: I have thought hard, down to my entrails. I reason thus: If a dispassionate thinker can clearly and distinctively conceive of a soul independent from a body, then it is necessary that the soul persists after dissolution of the body, because immutability constitutes the idea of the soul. I reason further than the soul's hunger for eternity exists only because there is an eternal being which satisfies it. More to the point, an eternal soul exists only because God creates it. Given that I clearly and distinctly perceive mind and body as independent, it follows that god exists!

Christina: WORDS! WORDS! You weave a net of verbiage, only to ensnare yourself in it, caught like a shark in a gillnet. You were right to say you should put these thoughts through your entrails. Think with your heart, Rene! Do you really believe that your dry logic will subdue your wild and staggering longings? God and eternity are not the last lines in a syllogism! I would laugh at your clownish efforts, were you not so tragically gifted and serious. Besides, your arguments are worthless.

Descartes: But the answers! What of the answers? Do they come or not?

Christina: They do not come! This is so tedious. (She picks up a book, looks, sighs. She then brushes her hair, puts on perfume, hums Chopin. He paces, reads from the treatise, mumbles, shivers.)

Descartes: You disrupt my lessons.

Christina: Save them. Help me brush my hair.

Descartes: How are they worthless?

Christina: God have mercy upon us.

Descartes: Where did I go wrong?

Christina: Help us in this hour of need.

Descartes: Proof! Give me proof! I pray for evidence!

Christina: PRAY? FOR EVIDENCE? You belong in a circus!

Descartes: Very well! I defer to you. Let us leave it here, and I will return to Holland. Good-bye!

Christina: What of the passions?

Descartes: (loudly). The passions matter nothing! They are negligible nuisances! There are no passions in heaven!

Christina: HEAVEN IS LOVE!

(Descartes and Christina both freeze, walk towards each other, Descartes shivering under the blanket. She touches him.)

Rene, abide here. Please, do not depart. Stay with me. You cannot go to Holland. There is ice on the water. You are sick in your lungs. I too live in the gloom of your solipsism, and like all solipsists I require company.

Descartes: Will you follow my proofs?

Christina: Proofs of what?

Descartes: Of immortality. Of the real distinction between the mind and the body.

Christina: Yes, I will follow them. (She starts putting on her gown. She does so slowly, frequently getting buttons and zippers stuck, almost comically.)

Descartes: Will you help me?

Christina: Help you how?

Descartes: Answer my questions.

Christina: Yes, I will answer them.

Descartes: What is corporeal nature?

Christina: I do not follow.

Descartes: What is the essence of the body? What is the nature of a physical thing? What is clearly and distinctly represented by the idea of an extended object, a bodily, corporeal thing?

Christina: I cannot answer.

Descartes: Think! (He pulls out a piece of her hair.) Look at this. What is its essence?

Christina: I can see it.

Descartes: Now turn your back to it. What is its nature when you do not see it?

Christina: It has solidity. It has a shape, a smell, a taste, it makes tiny sounds when I strike it…it feels…it feels soft…it dances on my neck in whispers…so soft…it is music…

Descartes: What else?

Christina: Sometimes it grows. Sometimes it's cut.

Descartes: So it is made of smaller parts. Does it think? Does it feel? Does it doubt?

Christina: No, its complete nature is to be thoughtlessly extended in space. It is pure matter. Never mind. It is only matter.

Descartes: It is extended, unthinking substance. What of your toe nail?

Christina: The same.

Descartes: And this? (Holds up the dumbbell. She nods.) And this? (Points to skeleton, she nods.) And when it was living? Were all the muscles material things? (She nods. He becomes animated.) And its organs?

Christina: The same.

Descartes: If I extracted a cell from its brain, would it also be a material thing? (She nods "yes".) Would you find thoughts in it? (She nods "no".) Doubts? (Nods "no".) Feelings? (Nods "no".)

Christina: No, it is just another part of extended, unthinking substance.

Descartes: Christina?

Christina: Yes, Rene?

Descartes: Would you think for me?

Christina: I am thinking for you now.

Descartes: Think of your hair. Does your thought of your hair have a colour?

Christina: No, my thought has no colour.

Descartes: Can your idea be tasted?

Christina: No, it is tasteless.

Descartes: What of the shape? Does it weigh anything? Can you smell it? Can you cut it in half? Can you show it to me? (Christina continues dressing. Descartes' animation rises.)

Christina: None of those.

Descartes: Where is your idea?

Christina: In my mind.

Descartes: And your memories?

Christina: In my mind.

Descartes: And where is your mind?

Christina: My mind is nowhere. It is unextended, as are its contents.

Descartes: What it its nature?

Christina: Its nature is to think.

Descartes: Yes! It is substance with no extension, whose sole essence is thought! I embrace you again! You are superb. You see? The body is unthinking, unextended substance. They are different natures! They are distinct. They are independent! (Descartes coughs, stumbles, dances, punches the bag.) One may exist without the other!

Christina: Are you finished?

Descartes: There are more steps in the proof!

Christina: (Quickly, impatiently) It won't work.

Descartes: But it is not yet complete!

Christina: No matter. You have fallen off the first step. The problems are legion. You wanted to prove immortality through God. You failed. Now you are trying again to reason from your ideas to reality. But every one of your ideas may be the murmurs of some insane delusion, or the contrivances of an arch-deceiver. You may also be dreaming. Don't you see? You have made it impossible, by the very conditions you laid down to achieve certainty, ever to get out of the pit of doubt you have dug.

Descartes: Christina…I…I…you…you…

Christina: Moreover, even if soul and body are distinct, how is the soul's immortality guaranteed?

Descartes: By God. That's right, by God.

Christina: And if they are so separate, how do they affect each other? How can they possibly interact?

Descartes: They co-mingle. Here (Points to the centre of the skeleton's skull)

Christina: (Picks up a ruler, points to its genitals.) If they interact anywhere, they interact here. Right here. (Taps her groin.) Right here. (Taps Descartes' groin.) Or here. (Touches Descartes' chest.) Or here (Fondles her breasts.)

Descartes: No here. (He puts his fingers through the skeleton's eyes.)

Christina: They don't interact at all. You have just informed me that a mind cannot exist ANYWHERE because it has no position, no extension. So how can it interact here? (Points to her head.) Or here? (Points to her groin.) You yourself made it impossible. And can you really think of your mind, you, your soul, the spirit of Rene Descartes, independent of your body, without your eyes, without your skin, without your ears, without your height, without your sex?

Descartes: The soul has no sex.

Christina: A mind alone? Without a body? It would have nowhere to BE. Where would it go? Would it do this? (She puts her hands in the skeleton, draws then out slowly, and flicks them in the air.) POOF!

Descartes: (Shaking) Give me one more night. I can think it through again.

Christina: Again, and again, and yet again. It will not work...It will never work.

Descartes: IT WILL! IT WILL! IT MUST!

Christina: IT WON'T! IT CAN'T! Your proofs are all demolished.

Descartes: So I have failed again.

Christina: No-one fails who fails heroically. (Descartes begins sobbing, and curls up in her arms.) Some women, the best of them, love some men, the best of them, who battle with heaven and hell, with life and death, when it is established from the outset that they are attempting what is impossible. Some of you are Saints, some Philosophers, some Poets, some Madmen, and some Lovers. Some of you are Weeping Clowns. Some are all at once. The heat of your burning touches us. All we ask is that your incandescent rage and fury...your luminous suffering…that the glow of your joy…that you…that I … that your abundant love…I have fecundity…that it shine on one of us…that the others stay in shadows. Dream your fevered dream…beside me…through me…to the last sad shudder…until it is done…and the dream is over. (Lights to black)

SCENE TWO

Christina is in bed, reading, wearing her bikini and tiara.

Christina: (Reading) "The utility of all the passions consists alone in their fortifying and perpetuating in the soul thoughts which it is good it should preserve, and which without that might easily be effaced from it. And again, all the harm which they can cause consists in the fact that they conserve others on which it not good to dwell". (Enter Dancer)

Dancer: It is well past midnight, your highness.

Christina: Ah yes. The dance. Melodic movement. Poems without words. The single speechless act...moving prayer...If only he...a waltz for two...one unspeaking gesture...dancing, dancing death away in a dream-dance...the lovers make the music...the music moves them...they dance to no words and become light...rising... merging...riding the harmonies of touch and taste...fleshly syllogisms...pinkish, watery logic...the perfect argument...vibrating...true and sweet...humming...(softly) and then the silence...the last chord struck...

Dancer: I am learning.

Christina: (Gets out of bed. Chopin music up. They dance in unison, effortlessly, then Christina falters.) I cannot finish. I never could. It is a furnace fuelled with snow...

Dancer: Have the men...were they...did they...

Christina: They tried. They were adequate. I was not. I let them rummage and glisten…their sliding syncopation would…it would…that elusive little pea in a meaty, folded pod…it…it dreams the wrong dream…you are not the dream… and I do not sleep…I need…(Enter Servant)

Servant: Madame, Monsieur Descartes is arriving.

Christina: How is his health?

Servant: The word throughout the castle is that he is gravely infirm. The consumption is setting in. He moves in and out of delirium. He now believes he is perpetually dreaming. (Exit Servant. Enter Descartes, shivering, wrapped in a blanket, hair wet.)

Christina: (Runs to Descartes. Embraces him. Puts him on the bed.) Rene, you are so ill.

Descartes: My reason is restored. God has seen fit to revive it, so I shall listen to its dictates and take the bleeding advised by your doctors. Christina, I am in sore need…my infirmity is…is part of the nightmare…the vapours are disordering my soul…my soul is…my infirmity…the grip of reason opens and closes but the dream goes on. (Christina gestures to Dancer. Christina and Dancer lie down on the bed beside Descartes.) I am not here. This is not me. I am someone else, dreaming I am here. Everything I say and think is someone else's dream. Who am I? Who is the dreamer?

Christina: The dreamer and the dream are one. This is all there is. (She picks up a sponge and mops his brow.) This is the life you are living. There is no other. It could not be otherwise. The God you adore must have decided it long ago.

Descartes: Ad gloriam Dei.

Christina: Do not pray.

Descartes: I hear angels…a ghostly choir…they will receive me…Pleni sunt coeli et terra gloria tua…I am drunk with his love…Domine, Domine, libera me…Lord, Lord, deliver me…

Christina: Rene, do not leave us. There is nowhere else to go.

Descartes: God is speaking to me.

Christina: No, my love. I am speaking to you. Savour your dreams of God if you must, but stay with us.

Descartes: I am certain….

Christina: There are no certainties. Except this. (She kisses him on the lips, gets under the blanket. Dancer exits.) Where is that gland you spoke of?

Descartes: Here. (He points to his head. Enter Servant)

Servant: Your highness. Your highness?

Christina: What is it?

Servant: Your highness. Word has reached us that Elizabeth of Bohemia, Princess Palatine, is making haste for Sweden and is due to arrive presently. She knows of Monsieur Descartes' condition.

Christina: How do you know this?

Servant: A letter through the Emperor's courier.

Christina:	What does it say?
Servant:	It says that Descartes had warned her he would die if he came to Sweden, and that she now makes great speed to be with him. (Exits)
Christina:	Who is she, most precisely?
Descartes:	A mesmerising mind. And her body is comparable to those which painters gave to angels. She melted my reason...I could have...her small white hands would open the gates of paradise...I dream of harps and little beams of light...
Christina:	Did you teach her philosophy?
Descartes:	Yes. She ruined me. Her hands...her fragrance...my arguments unravelled...
Christina:	It was the mind and the body, wasn't it? That was the problem. She did not let you divide them. Any good woman would do the same. They are not distinct.
Descartes:	But I clearly and distinctly perceive them to be...to be...Christina...just to be...or perhaps I do not remember...wrapped again in this dream...the hands...they were so clear...or was it?...is it now?...is it distinct? I do not now dream. No, I dream in another dream. Are you there? I remember the fragrance with great clarity.
Christina:	Yes it is all so clear. (She mops his brow.) Be still.
Descartes:	The pains are rattling like snakes. It is almost finished. I am so small. The great canvas of heaven, it stretches so far...It has sounds, it has fragrances...they happen all at once...this

epiphany of the senses, but they deceive me... they deceive me. "I suppose, then, that all the things I see are false; I persuade myself that nothing has ever existed of all that my fallacious memory represents to me..."

Christina: (Explosively) Rene! For the love of all that moves and lives and has being! Stop! For God's sake, for my sake, stop and love me, if only for one day! (Softly) Take succour, and I will give you rest.

Descartes: Requiem eternam.

Christina: Yes, eternal rest.

Descartes: He suffered. He was buried.

Christina: I suffer. I will be buried.

Descartes: Pecatta mundi.

Christina: The sins of the world. There are none. Only mistakes.

Descartes: (Whispering) I am so small. God is so great...Exalted in Love...majestic...the first cause...I clearly and distinctly...

Christina: (Soothing) Those thoughts are demolished. You yourself did it.

Descartes: A lasting and firm foundation for the sciences...

Christina: The greatest of all science is that of knowing how to live and how to die well. All others are useless if they do not contribute to this end.

Descartes: This wintry wasteland...Dei, Dei, pleni sunt coeli...

Christina: Yes, Heaven is full...is near...give in to it...it is love...it is MY love...

Descartes: (Still whispering) So fragile, so fallible...

Christina: So finite...

Descartes: So feeble, so feeble...I feel... (Descartes passes out.)

Christina: Schluter! (Screaming) Schluter! The cups! Bring the cups! It is not time for him to go! Quickly! Rene, do not leave! The lessons have just begun! (Enter Schluter and servant with the cups.)

Schluter: They are warm. (He and the queen roll Descartes over and apply the cups.) Can he be revived? It is now several days.

Christina: He must be.

Schluter: The delirium, is it in his whole body?

Christina: Yes, the misery is lodged everywhere. Fevers move in and out of his brain. (Still applying cups) More cups! (Schluter runs out.) It is not time. I am about to teach and learn. His mission is still before him and so is mine. His God cannot take his soul...his magnificent, omniscient, omnipotent, omnibenevolent creator would not do this...not if he loves us...(Enter Schluter with more cups)...not if he is perfect...but it does not matter...He does not exist...

Descartes: (Mumbling) Ad gloriam Dei.

Schluter: To the glory of God.

Christina: QUIET! Forget God. If he exists, he will let us be human. So let us be human. (Mops Descartes' brow)

Servant: There is no God. No perfect being would create imperfect beings like us, with such appetites for knowledge and truth, without providing us the means for satisfying our thirsts and hungers. If God exists, he is a sadist. (They all look aghast at her.)

Christina: Who told you that?

Servant: He did. (She turns to Schluter, approaches slowly, gently fondles his face.) And I in turn told him what to do without God.

Schluter: It is true. God could not be such a monster. He would not allow such urgent wishes for clarity and for direct impressions of truth and at the same time create us so imperfect that we are prohibited from ever achieving them.

Descartes: (Whispers) Faith. Faith will reveal...

Servant: Faith is an admission that reason has failed.

Descartes: It has not failed...it is divine...IT DOES NOT FAIL US! WE HAVE FAILED REASON! OUR RESOLUTION MUST BE TO USE OUR KNOWLEDGE AND WILL...(louder) ALL THE STRENGTH OF OUR INTELLIGENCE...TO UNDERSTAND...TO LIVE IN THE LIGHT OF...THE LIGHT OF...THE LIGHT...the swooning...lux eternam...eternal and precise...it is shimmering there...while I am mercifully in its aching love...I am dumb, I am blind, my ears are empty...

Christina: You are dreaming.

Descartes: It is there so full, so empty, and I am in the light of, the glorious light of...

Christina: Of love.

Descartes: Of love...

Christina: God is love.

Descartes: God is love...

Christina: I love you.

Descartes: I love you...

Christina: This is my body. I give it to you.

Descartes: This is my body. I give it to you...

Christina: This is my blood.

Descartes: This is my blood...

Christina: These are my hands.

Descartes: These are my hands...

Christina: This is my breath.

Descartes: This is my breath...

Christina: This is my dream.

Descartes: This is my dream...

Christina: I am your dream.

Descartes: I am your dream...

Christina: Please do not go.

Descartes: Please do not go...

Christina: Into your hands...

Descartes: Into your hands...into your...(Christina holds his hands)...hands...your hands of this...of this time...this time...all those memories...all those times...I commend my, my dreams, my fragile dreams of some mysterious place and time, where there is light so clear, so distinct, that you and I will think...will think we are dreaming a perfect dream... I think, therefore I ...it follows that I...

Christina: That I dream.

Descartes: I dream...

Christina: And if I am indeed deceived...

Descartes: ...indeed deceived...

Christina: ...I nonetheless exist...

Descartes: ...nonetheless exist...

Christina: ...So I am a real thing and really exist...

Descartes: ...really exist...

Christina: But what kind of thing? I answer...

All: A thing which dreams...

Descartes: ...Which...dreams...(smiling)...which... dreams....which dreams (Christina mops his brow)...which dreams (Descartes passes out, Lights to black.)

SCENE THREE

Descartes is alone in bed, shivering. Christina enters as he speaks.

Descartes: My soul, you have been captive for a long time. Now the hour has come when you must leave your prison, this body. You must bear the separation with joy and courage.

Christina: Rene, it is not your body which imprisons you, but your thinking.

Descartes: I know the hour is late. I have so little time. I fear I am at the final hour.

Christina: You are. The doctors have given you until morning. However, your life will be measured not by its length, but by its virtue. And it should have been a useless one if it had not prepared you for this moment.

Descartes: I am prepared. Let heaven receive me.

Christina: You are not prepared. WE have not finished all the lessons. Is the fever abated?

Descartes: God has granted me some respite, but it is returning. I feel it everywhere. I no longer know when I am in it. I seem to move in and out of dreams. I am not certain where I am or who I am. But it matters little. Whatever it is, it is slowing down, and spreading out. Words leave me and enter me but I do not know if I discern them correctly. I have thoughts, and opposite thoughts, but they all seem the same...bobbing on some ocean of uncertainty...my senses perpetually deceive me...or perhaps they don't...I do not know any more...the doubt is so severe that...that only God...the very God...the living God...more certain than mathematics...take me...I am being taken...his will is being done.

Christina: This is your last lesson. I will teach it to you. Nulli est homini causa philosphandi nisi ut beatus sit.

Descartes: Come near, Elizabeth. (Whispers) The proof...I am so sorry...I promised you...Elizabeth...to give you the proof...

Christina: (Mops his brow soothingly.) I am Christina. Elizabeth is downstairs. I am your proof. (Softly) Listen to my words. You have given them to me. I read all the lyrics you wrote for my dance...this is my dance...

Descartes: The dance? I came with proofs, and you, and you...

Christina: (All whispered) Yes, I know. But your proof was poetry...poetry for the music, for the dance. That is what you taught me. Now listen to the poetry...we shall start wherever we wish...that is called the beginning...it shall be gentle and quiet...a real beginning which few can endure...it shall be truth, and the truth will be beautiful, and it will hum a lullaby to you and it will comfort you... an exquisite, soft dance...moments and movements in my words...in your words...God's thoughts delicately dancing through you, beside you...just some beginning, a place to start...gentle, quiet, comforting...like a sleepy forest...like a slumbering mountain...like a mother's womb (A bit louder, but still a whisper. He is resting quietly. She removes his shirt as she speaks.)...just a silent beginning...calm and forever...leaving so much behind...letting so much go...until you find your certainty...resting assured... resting silent and certain...peaceful and comforted... easy, easy my love, it is all so easy...listen to the music (Picks up book) "It is now some years since I detected how many were the false beliefs that I had from my earliest youth admitted as true"... From your earliest youth... you have loved too much...so you were lonely...it is so easy to listen to me now...you loved like a God, and God is a bachelor...you never married...you were in love with truth...those who love truth distrust everything...follow me gently...we are dancing on words... your words... gliding to wherever they take us...so you doubted... (reads) " I was convinced that I must seriously undertake to rid myself of all my former opinions"...the bedrock of certainty...you wanted it... so you doubted your senses...like a lost child doubting the warmth of any mother's milk, unsure of a place, homeless, a brilliant orphaned mind, deceived by your eyes and your ears... betrayed by your memory, but still needing, loving, desiring truth... "It is sometimes proved to me that these senses are deceptive and it is wiser not to trust entirely to anything by which we have once been deceived." And you were wise. You were a youth, a foundling soul...the world was not safe...there was no soft breast to dream at...it deceived you...words fell apart, touch turned to cinders, the milk always turned sour...your love struggled with hope...your faith was betrayed...but incessantly you scoured the unfriendly world for love...you began to think: It must be there... and the more you ached...

the more you were deceived...the more you thought: it must be so perfect and secure that you will never find it...you loved truth and you begged for certainty, so much so that you made it impossible to find it on this earth...and you would never again be disappointed...you left your senses...you invented a world with no sounds, no smells, no sights, no tastes, and no touch...you live in a world without them...Plato's world, where nothing but ideas exist... and you would never suffer again... reason was your only resource... you invented the eternal because time was killing you...you invented the infinite because finitude betrayed you...you invented heaven because earth abandoned you... you invented God because people deceived you... and you invented the soul because it was your only exit from the deception, the cruelty, the misery, the solitude, the emptiness, and the misery and the terror... but let this thought waft over you, before it is too late...feel the warmth of this thought...and do not stir or start...this is pure love speaking, and I am saying: They have all let you down...reason, the eternal, the infinite, God, the soul, heaven...they have produced in you more despair and suffering than that which they were intended to cure...Listen to me now. You are listening to love, you have heard it before, but you must trust it now. There is nothing else worth listening to (She strokes his hair.) We are only beginning...at the only beginning. There is no evil genius. You are not insane. This is not a dream. You can trust your senses. They are not deceiving you now. We will still learn together.

Music up: Terrega, Recuerdos de le Alhambra, on Liona Boyd.

Where do you want to begin? (He heaves a big sigh.) Ah, yes, with the oldest sense. Let me say hello. (She breaths on his face.) Smell my breath. It will tell the truth about me... let the sense awaken ... enjoy its purity and fullness...smell this perfume...smell my hands, and this decaying skin... and play with them... and imagine that you do not think...that everything exists only in one sense...in the sense of smell...reality is the sum total of fragrance and odour...that is all there is... and all there is to do is frolic in them, all at once... and slowly, gently... think of your world becoming more fascinating, more enchantingly complex...something new is emerging...a new layer... a new dimension...gently now, softer than an angel's sigh... taste the lips which breath the sweet smell of love...taste my skin... I will feed you... (She gets under the blanket astride him, and appears to remove her bikini and his garments. All movements are very slow and dance-like.) And let the world grow again...it is all there... this is not a dream...be as still as the sunrise...let the dawn bloom slowly...opening, rising...like the first crimson flush of...of...love on my cheeks...slowly, slowly, my love, let your eyelids open, and look at me... and I will fill your eyes with these colours and shapes. Drink in all these sights...Look...here in my eyes, and you will see what you have sought so long in solitude...look deeper, even deeper my love...it is there...yes, you see it now for the first time...keep it all in sight...there is more and it is real...you are not being deceived...this is not a dream...this is the sight of me, the smell of me, the taste of me...follow me Rene, and hear me...listen, so quietly, listen...silent...listen...silent (She turns his head, puts her chest on his ear)...it is my heart ...you hear my blood...you hear my movements, my red and milky movements...you hear my words...you ride the waves of my words...I...Love...You...you float with my movements...our last and first love dance... and THERE!... the most tender of touches...it is all so real... a waltz... of words... of breath...each thought a new chord...fragrant notes... and you can taste them... and you can savour them... this feast of oozing sounds...this place to rest...these whispering sights...this harmony of watery tastes... look at how I touch you...feel my words...and speak to me... you can speak to me... put your breath in mine...and love will so the rest... (She now whispers inaudibly for ten seconds or so. He whispers back in her ear. His head falls back on the pillow. She is whispering. Music up. Slow fade to black.)

SCENE FOUR

Set is dark.   Christina is seated in a semi-circle with Elizabeth, the Dancer, and the Servant. They are all in low-cut leotards, except the Servant who is wrapped in two towels, one covering her head, as if she has just showered. The set is now spare, in black. The only visible prop is a table, on which is a tiara, a book, the dumbbell and the perfume bottle.

Elizabeth: I see why you dance. I must practice further. But where do we go from here? I think it is all up to us. Reason is dead. The absolutes are dust. Others will try what he tried, but they will not succeed. They cannot succeed. I told him he could not succeed some three years ago, when I was only twenty. (They all freeze. They all sway slowly and moan with pleasure, rolling their eyes. There is a whooshing sound of wind. The table moves. They all snap upright, as they were waking up.)

Servant: Fairy dust. It felt like a passing shower of fairy dust. (Elizabeth cups her breasts and stares at them with a puzzled look.)

Christina: Your highness, did you love him?

Elizabeth: More than anything.

Christina: Did you dance?

Elizabeth: Never. The lessons were too consuming.

Servant: What did you teach him?

Elizabeth: Nothing. I wanted to be his equal. He taught me all I know. I learned philosophy. Listen to what he says: (She pulls a letter from under her leotard.) "In the case of your Royal Highness, no diversions of the Court nor that mode of education which ordinarily condemns princesses to ignorance, have been capable of preventing your study of all that is best in the arts and the sciences. But what enhances my admiration most, is that so varied and perfect a knowledge of all the sciences does not reside in some ancient doctor but in a young Princess whose countenance and years would more fitly represent one of the Graces than a Muse or the sage Minerva". (She holds the letter to her chest and begins sobbing.)

Christina: That is most estimable. You must excuse me, your highness. I must go, I really must go. I trust you will retain all he taught you.

Servant: Your majesty, where are you bound?

Christina: I am not bound anywhere. I am free. Nothing binds me. Not even this. (She fingers the tiara.) I am abdicating my throne. My reign is comical and futile…it is empty, and I am too full for it. All that is left is music…music and movement…to learn and to teach…wherever there is hunger, I will attempt its satisfaction. Where there is not, I shall arouse it. I am leaving. Good-bye. (Exits)

Servant: And you, your highness?

Elizabeth: Descartes left some problems unsolved. Only a few remain to be conclusively put to rest. (She looks at the letter and sobs.) I want to be the one to do it. I want to be as brilliant as he was (sobs).

Servant: In philosophy?

Elizabeth: Most assuredly. And in mathematics. And in physiology. And in meteorology and optics. And I want to revise his *Passions of the Soul*. It should not take long. He will watch me from Heaven. And you? What will you do now, as a common woman?

Servant: I must remain with her majesty. My child will need support. We will be itinerant. With respect, Madame, I too must leave. (Exits)

Dancer: You have heard nothing from me. You will probably hear nothing from me again except the sound of my moving feet, and I now move beautifully when whatever moves me is also beautiful. (Exits)

(Lights down, as Elizabeth stares at the table, sobbing, with a puzzled look on her face. Spotlight up on the table, focused on the tiara, perfume, dumbbell, and book. She removes the dumbbell. Exits. Chopin music up. Lights up SL and SR. Christina is sleeping in a chair SR, in her aerobics outfit, a gym-bag beside her. Descartes is SL, also in a chair, wearing an exercise head-band and a sweat suit, asleep with a Playboy Magazine on his lap. The spotlight is still up on the table upstage, while the rest of the set is black. Knock at the door. Both awake with a start.)

Descartes: Honey! That would be Liz.

Christina: Come in! Come right in! (Enter Elizabeth) Hi! How ARE you? How are things?

Elizabeth: (In an aerobic suit, with a headband) Great! Super! Are you ready?

Christina: All set. Let's go. What about the kids?

Elizabeth: They're at Junior Achievement. I tell you, I don't know. That instructor is off to Cancun for two weeks and I don't know how this project will ever get done in time for the exhibition. Oh, what a super outfit! Where did you FIND it? FABULOUS for aerobics.

Christina: Catalogue crap. They don't make 'em like they used to. See you later, honey. Don't forget the steaks. And my hair appointment at four. Be right with you. (Elizabeth exits.) Are you OK? Well, don't worry about it. Think positive thoughts. Remember what the counsellor said. Positive. Positive. You'll be OK. It's no big deal. OK, gotta run. (Picks up the bag, and a book falls out.) Oh, what's this? (She leafs through it.) I know…Jackie left it at the gym. I'll give it back to her.

Descartes: What is it?

Christina: Some textbook for some ridiculous extension course she's taking. Religion, or philosophy, or something like that.

Descartes: Oh yeah?

Christina: Yeah. It's weird stuff. (Reads) "Philosophy signifies the study of wisdom, and by wisdom is meant not only prudence in one's affairs, but a perfect knowledge of everything man can know, as much for the way he conducts his life as for the preservation of his health and the invention of all the arts and sciences. (Music louder. They both move behind the table.) Living without philosophy is like keeping one's eyes shut without ever trying to open them; and the pleasure of seeing all the things which our vision discloses to us cannot be compared to the satisfaction found through the knowledge that philosophy gives. (They read together.) This study is more necessary for the conduct of our lives than is the use of our eyes in guiding our steps." (Pause. Music full. All lights down except the spotlight on the table.)

Descartes: Oh, for sure. For SURE. (Holds spotlight until music ends. Lights to black.)

Dr. Sean O'Connell teaches Philosophy at Grant MacEwan College in Edmonton, Alberta, Canada. He is also a Chartered Psychologist and an APPA Certified Philosophical Practitioner with numerous acting credits in film and theatre. Among his many publications is *Dilemmas and Decisions: A Primer in Ethical Theory* (Harcourt Brace).